THE WORLD BEYOND THE GRAVE

Bishop Athenagoras Cavadas

The World Beyond the Grave

by

Bishop Athenagoras Cavadas

Translated by

Constantine Andrews

Holy Cross Orthodox Press
Brookline, Massachusetts 02146

(C) copyright 1988 by Holy Cross Orthodox Press

Published by Holy Cross Orthodox Press
50 Goddard Avenue
Brookline, MA 02146

ALL RIGHTS RESERVED

Cover design by Mary C. Vaporis

Library of Congress Cataloging-in-publication Data
Cavadas, AThenagoras
[Yperperan. English]
The world beyond the grave, or, The afterlife/
by AThenagoras Kavadas: translated from the Greek
by Constantine J. Andrews.
p. cm.
Translation of: To Yperperan.
Bibliography: p.
ISBN 0-917651-52-9 (pbk.)
1. Future life—Christianity. 2. Death—Religious aspects—
Christianity. I. Title. II. Title:World beyond the grave.
III; Title: Afterlife.
BT902.C3813 1988
236' .2—dc19
88-12786
CIP

Dedication

To my Brethren, the Greek Orthodox Priests
of America

Dear Brethren:

Twelve years of my parish life, like yours, but also five years of service in the offices of the Archdiocese, unfolded before my eyes, in panoramic and clear view, all the struggles that a priest has to face in carrying out the very difficult double duty which the inscrutable will of divine providence and the voice of our mother country has placed on his shoulders.

I believe that my dual capacity as pastor and as chancellor gave me the opportunity to become personally acquainted with the unfavorable conditions in which each one of you finds himself in desiring, faithfully and conscientiously, to carry out his duty. I believe that I now know more fully all the pathways which each one of you is forced to take, in desiring and endeavoring to at least come close to the goal which has been prescribed.

Maybe we are not too well armed and prepared for such paths, for such struggles, for such unfavorable conditions. But in that instance, a few good encouraging words between us once in a while would surely provide us with more courage, more strength, and more success.

With this conviction, and wishing to encourage you, my brothers-in-arms, and to express my brotherly compassion for your sincere efforts, I dedicate this study of mine to all of you with Christian love.

Archimandrite Athenagoras Cavadas

Table of Contents

Preface ix
Why the Need for this Study xiii
Introduction 1
Part One: Necessary Christian Presuppositions 6
Chapter One: What is Death? 7
Chapter Two: Justified Doubts 10
Chapter Three: Where Can We Find the
   Necessary Information 14
Chapter Four: Divine Inspiration of the
   Information that We Have 18
Part Two: On the Present Life 20
Chapter One: Physical Death 21
Chapter Two: Untimely Death 25
Chapter Three: Spiritual and Intellectual Pleasures ... 31
Chapter Four: Emotional and Aesthetic Pleasures ... 34
Part Three: Intermediate Condition of Souls 37
Chapter One: The Other World 38
Chapter Two: Hades: The Place and Life
   of the Souls 41
Chapter Three: Necessary Summary of Questions
   about the Preceding 46
Chapter Four: Is Untimely Death an Injustice? 49
Chapter Five: Are There Pleasures in the World
   Beyond Similar to those of this World? 54
Part Four 64
Chapter One: Rewards and Punishments
   in the Life Beyond the Grave 65
Chapter Two: The Source of Beatitude
   or Blessedness 71
Chapter Three: Does the Soul Progress
   in the Next Life? 75
Chapter Four: Explanations 80
And Now the Conclusion 85
   Notes 89

Preface

I believe and have often preached that the life of man, as complete as it may be on earth, can be supplemented only by death, and that the deeper we study the problem of death, the easier and the better we will solve the problem of life.

Unfortunately, neither the one nor the other happens, because death is the most ancient event which man has faced, as the result of sin in Paradise. And since then, although thousands of years have passed and millions have died and die continuously, this event, which is called death, has been dealt with by very few persons with the necessary seriousness, timeliness, and patience.

Furthermore, it is very sad that we Christians also tremble before the idea of death. And when finally it comes unrestrained and inevitably, we endeavor with improvisations and haste to accommodate the situation, thinking that if during the last moments of life the most sacred duties are formally performed, then the soul of the one dying will have been saved. I have experienced a deep sorrow from such misperceptions of our Christians. Last night, at exactly one o'clock in the morning, I received a phone call from one of our faithful asking for a priest to give Holy Communion to a sick person in the hospital. And when I expressed my wishes for recovery of the sick person, the caller answered: "He will not last the night; in a short while, he dies."

From this, I surmised that the fear of death is due to a lack of true joy and happiness in life. From eternity, we limit life to the few meager years we live here on earth. We have the idea that if we do not talk about death we are superior people, but in reality we become inferior. As humans, we deny the immortality of the soul thinking that we, in this way, might possibly extend our life here on earth.

Nevertheless, I doubt if there is anyone who would face the reality of death with the same disbelief with which he might have lived his life. Some years ago, President Franklin

Roosevelt discussed with the Minister of External Affairs of Russia, Mr. Litvinoff, the possibility of recognizing the Soviet Union. I visited him at the White House in order to ask him to intercede in favor of the suffering Church in Russia. Mr. Roosevelt said to me: "I would like to relate something to you. During our discussion, I suddenly asked the Russian Minister: 'Mr. Litvinoff, when you realize that death is nearing, will you have the courage, one half hour before death to continue disbelieving in God, in the future life, and in the immortality of the soul?' Mr. Litvinoff kept a melancholic silence."

So that we will not grieve in the same way "as others do who have no hope" (1 Thessalonians 4.13), the present book, *The World Beyond the Grave,* comes to speak to us and to reinforce our faith once again in the Lord.

This is the second book of the "Greek Orthodox Family Library" which the Department of Missions of the Archdiocese has published, and one year after the circulation of the first. And it has the same purpose as the first. In the same manner as the book, *Why Should a Devout and Good Person Suffer in Life?,* so also the present book intends to enhance the religious life of our Orthodox people, giving answers to anxious questions which daily arise, and thus bring comfort to the Christian soul.

From the title of the book, *The World Beyond the Grave,* it is inferred that the thesis is one of the most difficult and mysterious topics of our holy faith, but also one of the most beautiful which can satisfy a pious soul.

That which distinguishes this book, just as the first, is the artistic philological simplicity in expressing its subject. In this manner, the author interprets the very mysterious, deep, and dogmatic complex matters into a more delightful reading, analyzing them conversationally as if they were usual matters of everyday life. And thus, although on the one hand the reader is drawn so that he may pleasantly peruse the book, on the other hand, almost unconsciously he comes to possess precious religious knowledge which concerns our holy faith and the future life of human beings.

Preface

This book will be especially valuable as an aid to our devout priests and co-celebrants in their soul-edifying ministry in developing the topics which concern: the spiritual condition of souls, the responsibility of a person for his moral life, the reward of the just and the punishment of the impious in Hades, the good enjoyment of life, the spiritual development in Hades, the communication between the living and the dead, repentance, etc., all inductively analyzed and pedagogically expresssed.

The author of this second book of the Department of Missions is the same, the untiring Archimandrite Athenagoras Cavadas, chancellor of the Archdiocese and Editor of the *Orthodox Observer*. Certain chapters of this study were printed in the *Orthodox Observer* and were greatly appreciated by the readers.

This study was further developed and organized into a harmonious wonderful book, double in size from the first, and artistically printed.

We offer it to our beloved children of the Church with the warm recommendation that they study it because their souls have greatly to benefit from it. Our Lord taught that the soul is the most precious of all the goods of the world.

I congratulate the author with all my heart and thank him, not as my chancellor, so that it may not be construed that I write gratuituously, but as one of my clergymen, just as I would have for any other one of our clergy who might occupy himself with such an effort.

I congratulate him, because in the time that he has, limited by the multifarious services of the Archdiocese, he has succeeded in producing a work which enriches our meager ecclesiastical literature, and especially on this topic which induces such deep thinking and sweet thoughts and flights of the soul.

And I thank him because this endeavor is a great service to the Department of Missions, whose purpose is to increase the knowledge, to protect against false teachings, and to lead to true faith, without which neither good works are done, nor is salvation of the soul possible.

By his graciousness in dedicating this study to his beloved brothers in Christ and concelebrants in America, I felt a deep spiritual emotion. This act honors the author and our clergy who are worthy of such tender expressions.

Perhaps some of our clergy might be lacking in education in comparison to the clergy of other churches. But they have this in their favor — they have always kept the torch of faith lit and alive, with which, in the darknesses of illiteracy and with so many other human frailties, leads the Greek soul there where from the beginning it believed and philosophized that it is destined to live eternally.

May our beloved clergy, carrying this torch also, impart it to our Christians, contributing to the greater distribution of the book, *The World Beyond the Grave,* of our beloved Archimandrite Athenagoras Cavadas, my faithful and devoted co-worker, chancellor of the Archdiocese.

May these few words be the small reward, and the circulation of his book the satisfaction which he proudly and praiseworthily has produced.

In Astoria, the 26th of January, 1937

Archbishop Athenagoras

Why the Need for this Study

In the twelve years during which I served as a pastor in the communities in America, I was called upon many tens of times to offer the Holy Sacrament of Communion to dying Greek Orthodox communicants, either in their homes or in hospitals.

Yet, I experienced great bitterness in the fulfilling of this high duty, because almost always some relative of the sick person would be waiting in the hallway of the home or of the hospital to intercede before I could enter into the room of the person who was to receive Communion.

The purpose of this concern was so that the sick person would not know of my visit, and would not know that I went there to offer the sick person Holy Communion.

"Father," they would say, "Tell him (or her) that perhaps you came here to the hospital for someone else and, by chance in asking, you learned about George, that he is ill, and you passed by to visit him and say 'hello.' If he should think that you came to give him Holy Communion, surely he will die from fright." Or: "Now that you are going in to see Maria, Father, tell her, perhaps, that you came to ask why her children were absent from school on two Sundays, and unexpectedly you found her ill. If she should suspect that you came purposely to give her Holy Communion, she will die from fright."

That was the most usual beginning for performing the duty of offering Holy Communion to the dying. We began, in other words, with lies. I was about to prepare a Christian Orthodox person for the life beyond the grave and I was expected to use a most wretched deceit to do so. I was about to emphasize the need for moral cleanliness to a sinful person, as we all are, and to touch the very sensitive chords of spiritual consciousness at the most appropriate psychological moment for a human being, so that from the depths of the heart could be heard the harmonious hymn of confession and repentance, but then they would put manacles to my hands and a muzzle to my mouth: "If he suspects, Father, that you came to offer him Holy Communion, he will surely die from fright."

This echoed continuously in my ears every second, sometimes pleading and sometimes demanding, when I wished to tell the sick person how beautiful death is for a pious person; to tell him how beautiful the other world is when the soul goes to it relieved, unburdened from the weight of sin by repentance and confession; to tell him how much and how the thirst of the soul is satisfied in the rest of eternal life beyond the grave which tortures us in this world and we know not what we seek.

In this manner, not a few times, with the thought that if the sick person should learn the truth that he is dying, that would kill him, and with the entreaties of the relatives surrounding me telling me not to insist but come another time when they would call me, I would leave unsuccessful, denying my duty, a coward, and embarrassed.

After five or six hours, I would be informed that the sick person, who might have lived five, ten, or even twenty years without confession and without Holy Communion, had died, unrepentant, without Holy Communion. Or I would be invited a second time, and when I would go, I would find him completely unconscious and naturally I would not be able to offer the Holy Sacraments to the corpse taking its last breath.

And at other times, when I would embroil the sick person in a labyrinth of lies, I would trick him, while conscious, to accept Holy Communion. Thus, Communion was offered mechanically, not conscientiously, without the necessary preparation which should be made with full knowledge of the sick person that he is leaving the present life. In this manner, the sick person, confused by the fear of death, seeing death's shadow, was trying to avoid it, only with the foolish thought that he was not preparing for death (as if death was about to ask if he was prepared, otherwise he would return at a later time), but in reality the sick person would die without repenting. The only words, whose sounds were obliterated in the weakened senses of their hearing, were the following usual, insipid, stupid attempts to console, promises of relatives and friends of the dying: "You will get well soon, George, and we will go to the church picnic, and we shall eat and drink and dance with the beautiful girls. Hey, George?" And George would be dead at that very moment, taking with him to the next world as his only companion the bitterness that he was not able to go to the church picnic to eat and drink and dance with the beautiful girls.

This then is the unfortunate situation of those Christian persons who are terrified by the thought that death is dreadful and they leave this life unprepared spiritually, because they lose even the last opportunity, the so-called mortal. And, furthermore, instead of dying with the sweet smile of satisfacton on their immovable eyes at that last moment, they are full of hopelessness and their face is wrinkled with the cold aversion from the fear of death.

This study seeks to end or at least lessen this unfortunate calamity. Those who will read this book, I wish to believe, will form a truer idea about death. Instead of thinking of death as their terrible enemy, they will accept it, when the time comes, as a good-natured friend who will transport their soul with his small boat into the quiet waters of the "Acherusion Lake," and away to the beautiful land of the other world, where no misery of life has a place.

And the priests, often at the bedside of the sick, who do not find anything more suitable to say, are forced to relate different stories without interest, that have no place in the holy moments of the last preparation of the soul for the trip to the other world. They will find in this book words of comfort, words to console the hearts that are torn apart by the death of a loved one, words which will show them to be, in those moments, dignified ministers of the divine will.

The joy from my belief that this will be the result of the edition of this study is the only reward I expect for my efforts.

Introduction

> "Who knows if that which is called death is life, and what is called life is death." — Euripides

One of the most profound and important topics with which philosophy and theology have been and are still occupied is death. But the phenomenon of death, with all its consequences, is at the same time one of the most beautiful and passionate topics with which poetry, music, painting, and, in general, art have also been occupied.

And truly so. Because this cruel termination of life, which suddenly separates forever beloved and adored persons from this world, and tears asunder the hearts of those who love them and suddenly lose them, is natural, is human. It is something that strikes directly at the sentimental center which people, not knowing where it is within us, identify with the heart, whose throbs are influenced by the various senses and feelings.

In the matter of death, we find the rendering asunder of the heart as more justified. Only a week ago, in one day, at a particular hour, you had a beloved person before you or at your side and you were speaking, or you were playing together, or you were making plans based, for the most part, on sweet dreams for the future, or you repeated for a hundredth time recent events or old memories full of fascinations and your hearts were flooded with joy. And then, in one moment, all that collapsed before you, fragmented and in ruins, and you were in the hopeless position of closing his eyes, dead, motionless, dim, which like glass remained inexpressive before you. Those eyes which, until that moment, like an exotic nymph, reflected and personified your chaste love. To cross over his motionless chest his cold hands, which when you held them previously you were transported, even though for a moment, to other Elysian worlds. To close forever those lips from which came the fragrant breath which hundreds of time you felt ethereal in the kisses of parents, children, brothers, sisters, and spouses.

How is it possible for pain not to come from such a tearing apart of the senses? That pain of the rendering asunder of the heart often closes tight the teeth and the lips in a long silence of him who hurts and makes his body tremble and his eyes to stare in anger and frustration. But, for the most part, rivers of tears flood his eye and bring to his lips an abundance of words, words of complaint, words of emotion, words that have created the most beautiful works of literature, in all the languages, and throughout the life of humanity. And I label them "the most beautiful works of literature," because they express the pain of hearts torn asunder by death. Just as in the pure joy of the heart there exists an emotional beauty, in like manner, in deep pain, in its tearing down, there exists an emotional beauty, the beauty of pain. This beauty of pain of the heart is incomparably greater, more sympathetic, and more imposing than the beauty of joy. The imposition that this beauty of pain exacts is most obvious in our social relations.

Your joys, whatsoever they may be, will hardly attract the joy of your enemy with their beauty. In your joy hardly any of your enemies will rejoice. But in your pain, in the breaking of your heart, his enmity will hardly stand against the imposition of the imposing grandeur of the purity of your deep pain. He shall be attracted by it and will sympathize somehow. And the noble pains, which like the chisel of a sculptor carves and beautifies, so also death works on the human heart and always ekes out a special place for a beloved person.

And the younger the person is that death, like a thief, grabs from the bosom of those who love him, and the more that he depended on others in life, materially or emotionally, that much greater does the injustice appear to be. And that much greater sympathy do the persons suffer who are hurt by the trauma that his death opened in the hearts of relatives or friends. And, for this reason death appears much more severe to the eyes of our imagination.

Thus, our imagination, with eyes filled with tears from the pain of the heart, sees death as a living being, and, moreover, as a horrible skeleton with eyes like dark holes and hands and feet like the limbs of a dry tree, seared by fire, dressed in a white shroud, with a long sickle in his hand, and is sometimes called death and at other times "Charon." In poetry, in mythology, in paintings, in sculpture, and everywhere else that art describes death, he is represented at times as a rider on a black or gray, blind skeletal horse and at other times as a boatman in his boat, in a wide, dark current, transporting souls to the other side of the "Acherousion Lake."

Whatsoever is horrible and frightening, that the heart of man pained by death can imagine, is attributed to the harshness and heartlessness of Charon. And this does not occur only in our times or generation, or generally in the Christian period, which softened the human heart and filled it with feelings of tender love and compassion for every endeavor. Neither did this occur only in the times before Christ, where the thought prevailed as a certainty that death was an eternal loss, without a trace of consolation or hope, because the truth that the human soul is immortal and that man as a being is never lost has always had a dubious meaning.

There never was a time that death was not considered in the imagination of man to be a very terrible thing. The wildman of the forest agrees in this with the civilized man of the city.

The wildmen of the forests, as primitive peoples of barbaric times in every corner of the earth, who were fathers and mothers seeing their child in its last hours fighting with death because of sickness certainly did not know what it was and from where it came, grabbed their stone or copper axes and, with angry words striking out wildly at anything possible that would make noise and tumult, chased shadows in their cave or in their hut and all around them, endeavoring to chase away death who they imagined to be an evil spirit so that it would not take the life of their child.

This continues even today! With almost the same plaintive dirges with which the wildmen of the forests complained, civilized man laments the loss of a loved person. The same occurred ten or twelve thousand years ago, the same happens today, and surely the same will continue to occur until the end of time. In such instances, even religion, with, perhaps, its balm of consoling words, words of God full of hope and assurance, does not succeed enough to bring relief. Because, with the breaking of the human heart and deeper pain, it is not natural to rationalize and philosophize on the true meaning of death, in order to drown the overflow of emotion which rises from the depths and to offer arguments to oneself with inconsiderate calmness towards the pain.

Indeed, for death to appear continuously so cruel and so abominable, at the threshold of our imagination, many other causes also contribute. But no less among these causes is when someone dies prematurely, especially when one dies from some sickness or by an accident, because this person is given to the hands of death, usually with pain and agony. And even though death, as the poet says, "is a deliverer from pains and is not at all responsible for the agony of the sick or dying person," our imagination, nevertheless, loads all on the shoulders of death. And though, in the instance of sickness, as well as in unforeseen accidents, death arrives, as always as the last visitor to the victim, again our imagination attributes the evil to it. And we all have the phrase ready, "the unfortunate one died a very cruel death," even though, in reality, death is the stopping place, the end of every cruelty in life.

However, at other times, when the heart, engulfed with the continuous pamperings of fleeting time, leaves the eyes of the mind dry to see clearer the various phenomena in the universe and in man, it is worthwhile to give a searching

Introduction

look at that phenomenon which is called death and to form a truer opinion about it and not to think of death as such a cruel enemy of human existence.

Such a searching look, illuminated by faith in the divine light, we intend to make concerning this matter and its mysteries, projecting several questions and supplying answers from the Holy Scriptures and the life of the Church, which is known as Holy Tradition.

PART ONE

NECESSARY CHRISTIAN
PRESUPPOSITIONS

CHAPTER ONE

What is Death?

To this question, Christianity answers: "Death for man is a change of life." But just as this definition is a simple one, and we can express it with only a few words, so also in its essence, the reality of death, is a mystery that generates many problems.

The spiritual and the physical consequences of this mystery, which we call death, is very great and extensive so that our mind finds it impossible to conceive of the entire meaning of the consequences of death. And much more impossible is it for the mind to define and enumerate all these consequences exactly for him who dies as for him who remains alive and has before him the impression of death which no one can avoid.

Precisely because of this, that death is a deep mystery, great pain is caused to the hearts of those who remain and who love the departed and suffer because of them. But it also terrorizes the thought of each one who reasons, saying: "Today or tomorrow, surely, my turn will come — and then where do we go from here?"

That is the most common and usual question which, uninvited, comes to the mind of the illiterate as well as to the educated person, when they see before their eyes a dead body which will be buried. And in the confusion of thoughts, which struggle with questions and secret fears that prevail in the frightened mind of man, we arrive inevitably to some simple answers, which are:

"Nowhere. To the complete loss of our existence, to non-existence," answer some, who pretend to be all-knowing. "To the other world," answer those who are pious and humble.

(a) We do not know if those who say that when men die, they are gone forever prefer non-existence after death because, perhaps, their accounts with morals are not in good order, which the immortality of the soul requires. Others do not prefer this answer at all. They are terrified by the thought of their total loss; but they find and support this opinion as the most convenient solution to the mystery of death. However that may be, we shall not give an answer in this book, neither to the former nor to the latter for the following reason.[1]

Those who accept nihilism, i.e., non-existence after death, do not accept God either. And if they do accept that there is a God, they accept him pantheistically, that is, that God is the totality of the physico-chemical powers of the universe, i.e., nature. They do not believe in a personal God who created man and provides for him, as Christianity believes. This we shall not discuss either, i.e., since they are not justified. This, too, is a matter that does not enter into our present study, just as the topic of the immortality of the soul does not. In such a discussion, the Christian faith and its teachings would have absolutely no place, because the Christian faith is the belief that *Jesus Christ is the Son of God, the Savior of the human soul, which he redeemed by his sacrifice as the God-man on the Cross at Golgotha.*

In his teaching, Christ does not endeavor to persuade his followers that the soul is immortal. He takes it for granted, as absolutely and indisputably known. And on this recognized truth he defines the relations which that immortal soul should have with its Creator and, in its behalf, he imposes the moral life, i.e., moral principles for life. On the other hand, it concerns those things which, because of their unimagined magnificence, would be inconceivable for impoverished human understanding. How can one describe the delicate color of the rose to a man born blind, or how can one describe the beauty of the Ninth Symphony of Bethoven to a man born deaf?

Indeed, the manner in which I expressed this teaching is very brief, very abbreviated, but in these lessons many teachings shall be developed which are inseparably connected with it and, at that time, sufficient explanations will be given.

Yet even though discussed briefly, it is very clear that any discussion with those who do not accept a personal God is out of the question, since the basis of the Christian faith is that Jesus Christ is the Son of God, and, naturally, we take the existence of God as basic and without question; because it is impossible to comprehend the Son of God without God and, indeed, a personal God.

Consequently, an apologetical discussion of these questions "concerning the existence of God" and the "immortality of the soul" would be the same as a denial of my purpose, as if I, myself, would negate the purpose of my writing.[2]

(b) That man has an immortal soul. The teaching of the Church that the immortal soul is the true essence of the person, that is his total self, his being, his personality, the only unchangeable element of man, is his soul. And the body with which he co-exists in life on earth is perishable, changeable and, although necessary, yet secondary.

Furthermore, we shall consider it such, since our topic is concerning death which liberates the soul from the body and separates the soul from the body. And later we shall discuss whether they are separated from each other permanently or only temporarily.

CHAPTER TWO

Justified Doubts

Since we are about to examine the matter of death, which is a mystery, and the consequences it has, transferring human existence to another life beyond the grave, naturally we are not dealing with a concrete matter, or with something in which experience, or one or two trials, will help.

We are sure that death is not a person, regardless of how much our imagination, when it is drowning with the pain of a broken heart, unwillingly looks on death as a person. Or when we prefer, for the sake of consolation, to see death as a person who acts and wrongs us, and we question him and want to know the reason for his cruelty.

And since death is not a person and, naturally, is not a thing either, then death must be a condition or, better yet, an event, which causes a change in the condition of man. Death is only the momentary time element in which earthly life ends a human existence and a new life begins in the other world, without any interruption, even for a thousandth of a second, of the real existence of man.

Indeed, this is how we Christians accept death, because, according to the Holy Scriptures, we believe that after the death of the body, the immortal soul continues to exist. If the atheists or deniers of the soul do not consider the death of man to be different than the death of a dog or any other animal, this is of no interest to us.

That which happens, therefore, at this momentary time period of death is nothing more than that a human being is separated from his fleshly body which disintegrates into the earthly elements from which it was created, in order to be vested in a spiritual soul, an imperishable body. In this manner, after death one remains the same person, the same entity, but only as a spiritual being.

This is the teaching of Holy Scriptures, concerning death.

But even though this teaching is so clear and definite, and if someone should distort it, he is a heretic, yet this same teaching of Holy Scripture creates for us many questions which need supplementary information or demand that this teaching be eludicated more analytically and somewhat more satisfactorily for our minds. Without supplementary information, doubts remain in our thoughts, which often lead us to delusions and such misunderstandings of life in this world, that we very easily take to evil ways. But even if we remain on good, moral paths, it becomes very easy for us, seeking a solution to our doubts, to fall into heresy.

For example, we say: "Fine, we shall remain and continue as a spiritual being, a soul. But what kind of spiritual being shall we remain? Are we going to have some other body, which is ethereal? A body that is spiritual, but a body which is the soul, which will occupy the same space, large or small, in the universe?"

Furthermore: "Whether our soul has a body or not, will it exist in some definite place, a place common to all? And if it exists in some place, where is that place for that new life after death, the life of our soul? And if we should remain in some place, shall we remain in that place forever, from the time of our earthly demise and unto eternity? Or shall we go first to some temporary place with the hope or assurance that at some time we shall go to another better place? Or is there a danger that we might fall into another worse place?"

Again, another matter: "Will our being (soul) after death retain self-consciousness? That is the most important matter of all. This, and only this, is called immortality. In other words: Will our soul remember our former life which we lived in this world? Will it remember clearly our former joys and sorrows? Will it embrace lovingly, in tender embraces, our beloved persons? And will it sometimes, again, in the sweet remembrances of the past, remember conditions that have remained unforgotten in all of our earthly life? Or will our soul find itself in a chaotic forgetfulness, as if it were brought for the first time to existence out of nothingness and non-existence, as if it never belonged to a human being that lived physically at one time on this earth?

And again: "If we retain consciousness after death and remember the good persons and conditions of the former earthly life, what relation will our soul have with the souls of our loved ones who left this world before we did, or those who shall come after us, inevitably indeed, to the world beyond? Shall the same beautiful feelings of love and affection bind us there as when we and they were living here on earth?" And then: "What relation will our soul have with this world, with those who have remained alive, until they, too, will come to the next world, to the life beyond?"

The basis of Christianity as a religion is that the Son of God, having become man, was sacrificed for the salvation of the human soul. But the salvation which the Savior, with his sacrifice, underwent is not given to man without some terms, good or bad; nor is it enough to believe in Christ as the Son of God and that that faith be weak, a mere faith, a dead faith, a faith without obligations, a faith that anyone can have, since it does not cost anything to have it. Christian faith should be expressed by doing the will of God. Jesus said:

> Not everyone who says to me, "Lord, Lord," shall enter the Kingdom of Heaven, but he who does the will of my Father who is in Heaven (Matthew 7.21).

And the Apostle James added:

> So faith apart from works is dead (James 2.26).

And, again, Jesus, sending his disciples out to preach concerning salvation, said to them:

> Go, therefore, and make disciples of all nations, baptizing them in the name of the Father and of the Son and of the Holy Spirit (Matthew 28.19).

Relating this command with the words that Jesus said to Nikodemos,

Justified Doubts

Truly, truly, I say to you, unless one is born of water and the Spirit, he cannot enter the Kingdom of God (John 3.5).

We find that for salvation, the sacrament of Baptism is necessary, but also Holy Communion because for this, also, our Savior Christ explicitly said:

unless you eat the flesh of the Son of man and drink his blood, you have no life in you (John 6.53).

All these together, faith, works, and confirmation through the Holy Sacraments are called: appropriation of salvation; that is, salvation, which was given by Christ, the Savior, to become our possession, must be given with our cooperation (synergy) that we might be considered worthy of it by God. This is imposed upon us by Christ. And if we are indifferent or negligent in appropriating our salvation, which Christ grants to us, if, that is, in one of these we are lacking, either in faith or good works, or neglect sanctification through the Holy Sacraments, we shall be worthy of censure and punishment. Consequently, Christianity is a religion not only of faith, but also of morals and a sanctified life. For putting it into practice, there is the promise of reward, and if not, there is the threat of punishment. But neither the punishment nor the reward are given in the present life. They shall be given after death, as our Savior Christ said:

"Come, O blessed of my Father, inherit the Kingdom prepared for you from the foundation of the world . . . " and to the others: "Depart from me, you cursed, into the eternal fire prepared for the devil and his angels . . . " (Matthew 25.34,41).

CHAPTER THREE

Where Can We Find the Necessary Information?

With these matters which I mentioned in the previous chapter, it seems that death, which is not something concrete but only the beginning of a new condition of human existence, is a very complicated, as well as mysterious matter. All these questions that are raised about it concern a life for which absolutely no science has given us facts, proofs, or elements on which we can rely. And if one should appear so daring as to say some things (as the experimental meaning of psychic phenomena), that which they give us is absolutely doubtful and inadequate.

Therefore, for those matters, we cannot know anything, or at least have any idea, if they do not tell us, like a prophecy, what will happen after death, that is, if they do not reveal or disclose what will happen by divine revelation.

But Christians, when we come to talk about matters of prophecy and divine revelation, should be content mainly with the teachings of Holy Scripture and the Christian Orthodox Tradition. And when we say, *Holy Orthodox Tradition,* we mean only the Holy Tradition which enlightens us in all that Holy Scripture authoritatively tells us, and not whatever just any one considers Holy Tradition, like, for example, the pamphlets that are known by the titles: "The Epistle of the Virgin Mary," "The Epistle of Christ," or any such others that are foolish fables.

What does Holy Scripture and Holy Tradition teach us concerning the life beyond the grave?

The answer to this question is that Holy Scripture and Holy Tradition teach us very little that is clear and definite concerning life beyond the grave. The reason is natural, logical, and simple, the following:

All the teachings of Christianity, i.e., the doctrines

(dogmas) propose to teach man his relations with God and his fellowman. The purpose is very obvious:

    a. For man to know and to believe who is his Creator, his providential Father, his Savior. And his worship of God should be a sublime worship, spiritual and not pagan, not a worship with superstitions, and,

    b. In order to be able to apply the will of God in his relations with his fellow human beings during his life on earth; to do good and avoid evil, and be raised in this manner to a moral and humanistic level higher in quality; to be proven worthy of the heavenly Kingdom.

    With this, we understand that almost the entire contents of the Holy Scriptures and the truths that are revealed to man by them are intended to prepare him adequately here on earth for the heavenly Kingdom. From the above comes the conclusion that the salvation of man, besides the sacrifice of Jesus who as the God-man was sacrificed for our salvation, is appropriated by two elements, first, the word of God, i.e. the revelation of divine truths, and second, the appropriation of salvation by man which, as we said briefly, is his faith, good works, and his participation in the Holy Sacraments. All these together, i.e, the appropriation of salvation, we can name as: cooperation (synergism) of man in the salvation of his soul.

    From the moment of death, man ends for all time every effort for his salvation, for the betterment of his being, i.e, his preparation in this world, which occurred by cooperation of man with divine grace, ends.

    From the moment of death, a new condition begins for the human being in which the future of the soul is now solely in the hands of God.

    Since, therefore, the condition after death is, henceforth, a matter for God, and man has nothing more to do (whatever he did was done in this life), there is no reason for God to reveal to man all that shall transpire after his death. There is no reason why God should reveal to man all the details of the life which his soul will have in the other world. That would be information and knowledge about things which would not change in the least the condition of man just by knowing them from before he dies in his life on earth.

The essential and necessary information for him to know is that he has an *immortal soul, that his existence shall continue after death,* and *that, according to his cooperation with, or his neglect of, appropriation of his salvation, he will be rewarded after death or punished.* That much is sufficient for him. And if this is not enough to make him careful, even if he knows all the details of the life after the termination of his human existence, it will not help him.

This is the indisputable truth of which Christ the Savior assures us with his" Parable of the Rich Man and Poor Lazaros." The unmerciful rich man being in "torment" after death, said to Abraham, "I beg you, Father, to send Lazaros to my father's house, for I have five brothers, so that he may warn them, lest they also come into this place of torment." But Abraham said, "They have Moses and the Prophets; let them hear them!" And he said, "No, Father Abraham; but if someone goes to them from the dead, they will repent!" He said to him, "If they do not hear Moses and the Prophets, *neither will they be convinced if someone should rise from the dead"* (Luke 16.27-31).

In other words, if the impious on earth do not believe all that Holy Scripture says, that they will be punished after death for their wretchedness, then neither, again, if the dead would arise from their graves and tell them the details of the life beyond would they believe.

Recapitulating all the above, we repeat that if the great truths which God revealed in the Holy Scriptures are not sufficient for the Christians, even though there is little concerning life after death and the condition of human souls contained in that unique Holy Book for our salvation, then neither would ten other such holy books, if they existed, which would contain all the details of the conditions of souls after death, have the least influence upon them because as our Savior says, neither the witness of the resurrected dead

Where Can We Find the Necessary Information? 17

will be able to convince the evil and unbelieving person. The unbeliever and evil person, again, would doubt and reject the authenticity and sacredness of these books, just as he disregards the authenticity of the Holy Scriptures.

For this reason, in the Holy Scriptures, we do not have a sufficient, definite, and clear teaching on this matter. And not only for our existence after death do we not have details, but neither even for the time in which the Final Judgment will occur do we have sufficient information. Our Savior said:

> But of that day and hour no one knows, not even the angels of Heaven, but the Father alone (Matthew 24.36).

CHAPTER FOUR

Divine Inspiration of the Information That We Have

That God withheld, of his own accord, teachings concerning life after death and did not reveal all, not even to the divinely inspired Apostles and Evangelists, does not detract from, nor harm, the authority and the value of divine inspiration which the Apostles and Evangelists had. Divine inspiration is not all-knowingness. Omniscience is an attribute of the infinite and unlimited God alone. And divine inspiration, which the Apostles and Evangelists received, purposed to make known all that God considered necessary and sufficient for man to know in order that he could cooperate towards attaining his salvation.

The exact same thing occurred with the Divine Inspiration of the Prophets. The fact that they were inspired and saw visions in order to reveal some specific will of God to the people does not mean that they had complete knowledge of the unwritten book of all the mysteries of the Deity and of the invisible or spiritual world. From all that was said in the previous chapter, it is obvious that the great golden latticed door, through which the human soul passes to the life after death, is closed to the thought and the observation of man as long as he is in the present life. But it is not a wall that separates us; it has bars. And through the lattice-work, as dense as it may be, the eye of our soul, even from this world, can see a little of what is occurring or is being prepared to happen in the faraway place of that life, the eternal distance of the life of the soul. For such an observation and for our spiritual satisfaction, we shall make the necessary and indispensible combinations of verses from the various books of the Holy Scriptures, i.e, from the Gospels, Acts, and Epistles of the Apostles and the Revelation of John. With these combinations and some information from the Fathers of the Church on the scriptural verses which constitute the pure Holy Tradition, we will arrive at the desired answer, which gives us in this life spiritual satisfaction.

Thus, it remains, as a conclusion, that the answers that we shall give with this study to the questions with which the matter of death is surrounded, shall have the information which Holy Scripture and the pure Orthodox Holy Tradition give us. But even this information concerning the unknown mystery of death does not comprise an open door from which we can see the life beyond the grave, but only a latticed door whose bars are very closely placed so that between them or soul and thought, with our faith as a guide, can take a glance at the other life. But those glances, surely, are satisfying for our souls as long as we remain in our physical life.

And now, on this basis, let us proceed to examine our subject.

PART TWO

ON THE PRESENT LIFE

CHAPTER ONE

Physical Death

There are two kinds of physical death, natural death and untimely death.[3] Every living thing, animal, plant, and insect has a beginning and an end, with the difference that some have a life of short duration while others have a life of relatively long duration. For example, there are insects and plants whose life span is transient, i.e., they live only one day or only a few hours, while some trees and animals live for centuries. There are trees that are 500 or 800 years old or more.

They tell us the same about some animals, birds, reptiles, and sea monsters. Turtles live 200 years and other animals the same, more or less. The longest that a man may live, and even this occurs rarely in our times, is to the age of 100 years. It would be of great fortune if all people lived these 100 years and were satisfied, and if it were possible for them to remain in good health and with all their bodily functions intact. In other words, to have their sight, their hearing, to have their teeth, to be of sound mind, to be able to walk freely, etc. But these functions of the body, unfortunately, begin to weaken, under ordinary circumstances, from about the age of 55 years, on an average in healthy persons. Biologists tell us that from the 40th year the human body begins to irreparably deteriorate, but we find it hard to accept this because it would be too discouraging.

The remaining years, then, from 55 to 75-80 are often nothing more for man than a totality of troubles of physical misery, which are brightened only by a few short-lived joys.[4]

That which makes man tolerate this condition is the invincible natural, even though not always justified, hope of man that tomorrow will be better than today. Should we live, however, 80 or 90 years or even more and be, in our old age, blind or deaf or motionless in bed or in the sun or in a chair and talking or thinking childishly, often with pain, a burden to ourselves and to others, it would be better to figure that the preferable age limit of man should be seventy years.*

Regardless, however, how much we can extend our life or that of our dear ones, we are sure that after sixty, the end is drawing near. In that case, it would be inconceivable and unjustifiable to think that death is cruel, or that the Lord of life, God, is cruel, because an old man or old woman was taken at age seventy or eighty or eighty-five, and since, indeed, we expected it naturally, just as we await winter after summer and autumn and since, in essence, the old person has no real enjoyment in life other than the idea that he is alive.

There remains a separate enjoyment for the old man or old woman that they have around them, their loved ones from whom they do not wish to be separated. As much as Mr. Krenderopoulos tells us that the aged detest everything that has a youthful age and that they become misanthropes, the truth is that most of the old people sincerely and warmly love the son or daughter, the grandchild or niece or nephew from whom they do not want to be separated. One such idea or enjoyment that is natural and great, out of holy love that reigns in the sensitively polite hearts is justification enough for him who is dying to be sad even at such an age. However, the aged person that has no other satisfaction in life except the companionship of loved persons, when he leaves this life, will be going to another life where he will meet persons equally dear, and perhaps dearer, who died before him and, therefore, would not necessarily be saddened by the separation from those he leaves behind. And if that is true and, consequently, the loved persons that remain here and whose companionship is the ultimate purpose of the life of the aged person, too, will go to meet him in the next life sooner or later, then why would it be necessary to characterize his death as pitiful, either by the aged person that is dying, or by the others? What does he lose by death?

*Translator's Note: The above figures were true for the times this book was written. However, recent statistics show a far greater increase in life expectancy.

Furthermore, as a Christian, if he believes that the life to which he is going will be one in closer communion with Christ and God, from whom all true joy comes, as Saint Paul says in his Epistle to the Philippians: "My desire is to depart and be with Christ" (Philippians 1.23), then sadness for the natural death, either of him or the loved ones is not justified.

But we are not sure that the person of old age who is dying a natural death is truly saddened by it. He could welcome it and we may not realize it. Or sorrow may be written on his face because he undergoes a false feeling of sadness by reflecting the sorrow expressed continuously by those surrounding his deathbed. Or his sorrow may not come because life is being snuffed out, but because of the dreadful needling of conscience, from the dread of the memory of an unchristian life that such moments produce. However, since we shall speak of these matters later on, it will be proper, at this time, to merely examine whether there is a reason for loved ones who remain and express sorrow to be sorrowful, and whether the expression of their sorrow is pure, sincere, and polite.

And, actually, even those relatives and friends who truly are sorry on the occasion of natural death of a beloved aged person, a father, mother, uncle, aunt, etc., must confess that they are not facing reality, but are governed by an unexamined emotion.

Because if they had thought that the loved one dying of old age not only is not losing anything of value from life but, on the contrary, is liberated from the unavoidable wretchedness of old age, accompanied very often by a dreadful sickness, then they would find that if it is not natural to be glad when a loved one dies, at least it is not logical to be sorrowful.

And, furthermore, if, as Christians, they believe that the soul of their beloved aged person shall find itself beyond the grave in closer communion with Christ and God and, further, that he shall find himself in a condition from which not only "there is no pain, sorrow, and suffering" but is the fulfillment of the desires of a pious soul, then even if it is not natural to express joy, joy must be borne in their heart for that death.

But, as you see, we set down three "ifs." Are these "ifs" realities? That is what we shall develop, after we next examine untimely death.

CHAPTER TWO

Untimely Death

We explained sufficiently in the previous chapter that when the person whom Charon takes, dies a natural death of old age, then death is not cruel, neither for the person who dies nor for the loved ones who remain behind. We have in mind that this is true when we defend the three "ifs," i.e., the three hypotheses that we mentioned in the previous chapter, and which we shall explain later.

However, can we, therefore, say the same thing concerning death which is untimely as caused by sickness or an unexpected accident?

Can we say that death is not a cruel trial when Charon takes an angelic child with its innocent laugh that reechoes like harmonious little bells in the ears of a father and a mother who are enchanted by its love, and while its beautiful little hands which lovingly embrace them are giving them untold happiness? Or when Charon takes a brave young man of eighteen years who encompasses all the hopes and desires of his family? Or the young lady of equal age whose parents yearn and dream and await the blessed hour when they will kiss her wedding crowns when she marries? Or the mature man who, full of life and activity splits the stone and with his life he gives life to his house? Or the mature woman/ a mother who makes her family life a veritable Paradise with her judicious and untiring efforts for all?

All these persons, and many others who, as we usually say, have hardly yet eaten their bread of life, obviously have been cheated by an untimely death. And not only they, but also those persons remaining with hearts torn asunder, are cheated by the untimely loss of their loved ones.

In order to examine, however, if, in reality, in the case of an untimely death that an injustice has occurred, it will be better if we separate that person from the persons who remain behind with broken hearts and speak first about him.

It is true, as we all agree and repeat, that life is sweet and that in childhood, in early and middle age, there are beautiful and satisfying times which make life desirable and truly sweet. There are some presuppositions, however, in this connection, that we will mention in another chapter. At the same time, we must confess that only a few people are satisfied with their life and express their satisfaction in an unaffected manner, regardless of what kind of life they may have.

Almost everyone complains about their life. Some about their health; some about their work; others are disappointed with their families; others because of financial difficulties; and still others disappointed in love; some because of social failures; some for this and some for that reason. And if you show any interest in their troubles, they will describe their life as more unfortunate than anyone else's. Very seldom wil you hear someone relate their happy times, and if you do find someone who does, it will be after proper and technical improvised humor.

Indeed, if you should say to someone disappointed in life: "My Christian friend, since you are not satisfied with your life, why don't you commit suicide to get it over with?," they have a ready answer. Some will say that they are afraid of God and they don't want to lose their soul. Others say that they hope to have a better tomorrow. That may be so. But the greater truth is that the former and the latter desire to live because within us is the awesome power that imposes upon us a thousand ways to want to live. This power is the animal instinct of self-preservation which all living things have and which no one knows exactly in what part of us it rests. Truly, however, it does exist within us, and very few are they who can avoid it and commit suicide.

This power, the instinct of self-preservation, therefore, makes our life sweet with many lures, and not those lures which we call pleasures of life. Because, on the contrary perhaps, most of those pleasures usually have very adverse physical, moral, and social consequences that have a drastically wretched effect on life. For this reason, we say that a person is forced or is fooled by the instinct of self-preservation to love life, regardless of how many misfortunes he may have. We say the same about the animals.[5]

Therefore, it is really not true that, with an untimely death, a person will be deprived of the pleasures of life which we say make life sweet. But it is that unknown something within us which makes untimely death seem to be the destroyer of a life of pleasure, which we should perhaps enjoy.[6]

When, however, someone overcomes this strong instinct by reasoning or stubbornness, and commits suicide, we say in truth and we agree that that person was insane when he did it and did not know what he was doing, because suicide is an absolutely unnatural thing.

With this, I do not wish to say that life is not worth living. Neither am I a pessimst to think that life is unbearable. And when a person through stubbornness scorns this strong instinct of self-preservation and commits suicide, I believe and proclaim that that person found himself in a condition of insanity because, as I said, suicide is an unnatural thing. Furthermore, I assure everyone that suicide is the greatest sin of all, because the person who commits suicide, besides the fact that they terminated their earthly existence against the will of God, unconcerned if this was a trial for the good of his soul, they, at the same time, have forever eliminated every hope and possibility of repentance. Neither would I allow myself to criticize the work of God and let it be thought that life, which I strongly believe was given by God to man, is the work of the evil god Ariman and, therefore, evil and worthy of scorn.

On the contrary, I believe, as I said earlier and as I developed it sufficiently in my other book, that life has many pleasures. The only difference is which enjoyments we believe can make life truly worth living and, at the same time, make it such that it will enhance the life of the soul.

And to this specifically, I wish to give our attention, because precisely on this the entire solution of the problem depends.

There are, indeed, pleasures such as eating good food, drinking, physical satisfactions, dancing, taking trips, which even though they are conventional pleasures and they bring physical exhaustion, nervous overstimulation or breakdown, and spiritual weariness, we cannot deny that, at the same time or moment that they are being satisfied, they also give some pleasure.

But these pleasures are physical and common and similar with those of animals, the four-footed, the two-footed, the birds, and the fish. If those pleasures are such that their worth in human life is taken from them, then human life has just as much worth as the life of animals, birds, and fish. Consequently, the untimely or violent death of all the animals (slaughter, hunting) should be considered a crime just as much as the violent death (poisoning, murder, etc.) of humans is.

But such a thing as that, the slaughter of a lamb or catching a fish as being the same as the murder of a human being, is not seriously accepted by anyone, not only because we all eat slaughtered animals (for even Christ ate fish), but because something within us tells us and assures us that the worth of our life does not depend on physical enjoyments which are common to man and to animals alike, but on other more spiritual things which life gives. And if man's life is based on such animalistic pleasures, then again untimely death does not have the same meaning, just as slaughter of animals, the hunt, and fishing does not.

And if someone would tell me that man has physical and emotional pleasures which the animals do not have, as, for example, travel, music, the theater, the movies, dance, and other similar things, I would answer that these are not able to become the basis for the worth of life, nor do all people have them. On the contrary, indeed, many persons do not have these to enjoy, and yet they live a simple and serene life, incomparably sweeter than those who enjoy these things. And, furthermore, not a few of those who enjoy these pleasures and consider them capable of sweetening their life, yet throw it away by committing suicide.

And here is exactly what I wish to conclude and to make understood, that life truly has pleasures which make it enjoyable. With this difference, however, that the pleasures that make life truly worth living are not all those which man will lose when he dies an untimely death. Consequently, it is not true that death is cruel and unjustly comes at untimely moments, because, peradventure, it takes man from the pleasures of life. Such pleasures alone do not justify the existence of life — they are only means to sustain life, to be transmitted to children and grandchildren in order to perpetuate one's kind, just as it occurs among the lower animals. For this reason, we say that the person dying an untimely death is not cheated, is not deprived actually of anything or any pleasure if we consider enjoyments to be good food, drinks, and anything else that is common to the other animals. Because these are not pleasures of life, they are only the means for the sustenance of life and, in essence, are not necessary for real human existence, which is the life of the soul.

There are, however, some pleasures in the earthly life of man which also have a real value. But they are those pleasures which enhance and improve the life of the soul. For a true Christian who would want the physical pleasures if they enhanced the life of his soul, it is not a misfortune if he should be denied these, as long as he is not denied those things which concern the life of the soul. Therefore, if death will deny man the pleasures that concern the body or only his earthly life, and if they do not deny him the pleasures that concern the life of his soul, then for the Christian, death is not in the least an evil and he has no reason to be sorrowful when he dies young in an untimely death.

But here, too, we have based our argument on an "if," and later we must prove it also. To prove, however, that death does not cheat man in an untimely death, it is necessary:

a. to define which are those pleasures that concern the life of the soul, and

b. to prove that to deny man these pleasures of earthly life when dying an untimely death is neither cruel nor unjust, because he shall find them in the life beyond the grave.

The definition of the first matter could be given with only two phrases, i.e., the pleasures that make life truly worth living are the *spiritual* pleasures, the *intellectual,* the *emotional,* and the inexpressible pleasures that come from the beauty and grandeur of the universe and from the wonderful daily works of God and man, and which all together can be called *aesthetic* pleasures. We say that these enjoyments make life worth living because, besides being true pleasures in life, they furthermore enhance the improvement of the life of the soul.

We must further develop these two phrases and analyze them so that all may understand them better. But we shall not do this with scientific theories and details, nor with rhetorical descriptions in a sermonic manner. We must simply endeavor to make it possible for anyone reading this study to understand these matters.

CHAPTER THREE

Spiritual and Intellectual Pleasures

Educated people often do not make a distinction between these two words, *spiritual* and *intellectual*, as if they were the same word, or they may use one instead of the other. Even in philosophy, in history, in sociology, and law, the same usage is made. For example, when an author writes books, the others say that these books are spiritual productions of so and so which, in reality, are his intellectual products. Also, when a person has a strong mind, i.e., when he is clever or an intellectual, we usually say that that man is spiritual. In law, a person's intellectual work is characterized as his "spiritual property," which he wishes to commercialize. This confusion or unconcern about using one of these words for the other, as if they were the same word, happens because with the word spirit (*pneuma*), the various wise men have defined many and different things.

However, in Christian life, "spirituality" and "intelligence" are two separate things, each with a different meaning. Since the soul is a spirit, the higher powers of the soul are called the "spiritual" powers of man. And the spirituality of man is the tendency, the urgency, the desire of his soul to know God, to communicate with him, to delve into the divine teachings and to practice in his daily life the laws of God. In other words, the spirituality of a person is his tendency towards a religious and moral life. In the English language, the "*pneuma*" with meaning is called "spirit," and the "*pneumatikon*" is called "spiritual."

The intelligence of a person is an entirely different thing. Intelligence is not an activity or desire of the soul; it is an activity of the mind. The intelligence of a person is the ability of his mind to think, to understand, to comprehend those things which pertain to him and the world which he sees all around him. For example, the intelligence of a person is his ability to read and to write, to count, to learn foreign languages, to explain the natural phenomena, to combine chemicals or other phenomena, to invent and to use tools and machines, to philosophize about the invisible and abstract, to judge, etc.

In the English language, *"dianoesis"* is called "intelligence," and a person who has "intelligence" is called an "intellectual," and the word "intellect" is never confused with the word, "spiritual."

Consequently, the spirituality of a person, i.e., his religious and moral condition, depends on his intellectual capability. For example, a small-minded or feeble-minded person may be in the dark concerning religion and morals; because of his limited intellectual ability, his mind cannot comprehend them. However, as much as intellect or spirituality might depend sometimes on the other, they are different one from the other. A person may be very spiritual, i.e., pious and moral, and yet his intelligence may be very low, very poor, so that he may not be able to solve a simple problem in arithmetic. Or you may speak to him about the same thing for an hour and he may not understand you at all. On the contrary, a person may have great intelligence and be a great scientist, in general, an intellectual, and yet he may not have the least spirituality and even be an atheist and immoral.

I believe that up to this point we have made it clear that the spiritual powers of man are something different, from a Christian point of view, than his intellectual powers are. In the same manner, we can separate the "spiritual pleasures" of a Christian from his "intellectual pleasures." Examples:

The true Christian finds spiritual pleasure in his faith and his reverence toward God, in his moral improvement, in his efforts to teach and convince his friends to believe and become good persons, in reading religious books, in prayer, in receiving Holy Communion regularly, etc. All these are "spiritual pleasures" for the Christian.

A person finds intellectual pleasure when he can extend the horizons of his knowledge and thoughts; when, from a certain given, by research, observation, or thought, he finds something new in philosophy, in the various sciences, in mechanics, or elsewhere.

All these are "intellectual pleasures" and, because of them, many devoted persons not only have sacrificed the physical pleasures of life, but even life itself. In this matter, however, it is necessary for us to observe the following: Even though the spiritual pleasures are all good and promote the life of the soul, the intellectual pleasures do not all work for the improvement of the life of the soul.

As we said above, an intellectual person may be impious, atheistic, and immoral. For this reason, when we say that a Christian has intellectual pleasures, we mean that he should be conscious of his insignificance in comparison to the incomprehensible grandeur of God, so that when he studies, thinks, experiments, philosophizes, and finds pleasure in all these, he should not imagine that this is the entire purpose of his life. Nor that with these things he has conquered the universe and dominates over it. In these devout pleasures, he should not consider himself greater than God and imagine his science to be omniscience — all-knowing, or his ability to invent to be a substitute for the miraculous powers of God. If a person limits himself to within the boundaries of piety, i.e., if he does not regard himself too highly, and with his intellectual accomplishments he does not imagine himself so great that he does not take God into account, then his intellectual pleasures are truly pure pleasures which enhance his earthly life and the life of his fellowmen, but also the life of his own soul.

CHAPTER FOUR

Emotional and Aesthetic Pleasures

Then we have the emotional pleasures. For the good Christian, they could be included among the spiritual pleasures because emotional pleasures result from the practice of Christian morality, which is a matter of the soul, that is, a spiritual matter. For example, the love for neighbor, charity, self-denial, love of parents for their children and spouses for each other, visiting and consoling the sick, etc. give true and beautiful pleasure. All these, indeed, are pleasures that come from Christian morality and, consequently, are no less spiritual pleasures. However, those who practice morality only philosophically, such as Socrates, Cleanthes, Epictitus, and other ancient or modern philosophers and humanists, have these same pleasures, without being Christians.

In our present study, we are considering only the religious Christian pleasures, as spiritual pleasures, which arise from our relations with God and his only-begotten Son, Jesus Christ. For this reason, I have separated the pleasures that are the result of our good relations with other persons, our neighbors, and have called them emotional, which even the non-Christians may also experience.

Lastly, I mentioned the pleasures that arise in the soul of man from the wonder of seeing and examining the works of God in the universe. We can call these aesthetic pleasures because we experience them through the senses, without using our thoughts or emotions. For example, a dark green valley embroidered with multicolored flowers imparts aesthetic pleasure. The moon-bathed night with sweet reflection in the sea, while the zephyr makes it shiver with its tender caress as it moves slowly here and there, gives aesthetic pleasure. The singing of the lark in the forest at night or the harmonic symphony of birds at the break of day gives aesthetic pleasure. The musical harmony of human voices

Emotional and Aesthetic Pleasures 35

gives aesthetic pleasure. The rising sun or its setting in the ocean with a clear horizon imparts aesthetic joy. A mountain range reflected in a lake like a crystal mirror gives aesthetic joy. The ripe wheat stalks in the fields yellow like gold coins and the trees bearing multi-colored ripe fruit give aesthetic pleasure. The fragrant breeze from the sweet-smelling flowers of the cultivated and the wild trees, bushes, and plants gives aesthetic pleasure.

We can mention hundreds of other aesthetic pleasures which give true pleasure to life and enrich the life of the soul, because when we admire the beauty of nature, there is nurtured within us the feeling of reverence toward the Creator and, consequently, our hearts are filled with devotion and gratitude. The Christian has similar aesthetic pleasures from admiring human inventions. The Christian, seeing the many surprises that the science of electricity presents to us which help us to discover natural laws which were unknown to the people of yesterday, cannot but admire the omniscience and omnipotence of God. This admiration creates within him great pleasure. For example, when one stands in front of his radio at home and hears an orchestra playing in another place two-three thousand miles away, he feels a great and pure pleasure from the idea that God set such laws in the universe so that two metal combs and two or three tubes are able, with the assistance of electricity, to capture the sound waves of faraway orchestras and reproduce the sounds and the harmony exactly as they are played there. The same occurs with the light waves, the radio, television, etc. And now we repeat the question:

"Isn't untimely death cruel, since it denies man such pleasures, taking one away before he could enjoy them fully?"

And we answer: "It would certainly be cruel if a man dying an untimely death was himself, his soul, his being deprived forever the pleasures of life. But if, in the life beyond the grave, the human being, now a soul freed after death from the body which often, because of misfortunes, hinders such pleasures, has and feels these pleasures more strongly, more acutely, more beautifully, then we can say that it is completely unjustifiable if a Christian dying an untimely death, at an early age, is sad because of it.

Again, we stated two "ifs." That is, *if,* in the life beyond the grave, such pleasures exist there and *if* these pleasures can be felt there by the soul, and indeed more beautifully, livelier, and eternally.

The assurance of these two "ifs" also shall comprise the contents of the following chapters. For this reason, we will begin with the question: "What remains of our being (ourselves) after death?"

PART THREE

INTERMEDIATE CONDITION OF SOULS

"Those who think that the natural consequence of life, the exodus from this life, is a calamity they deeply mourn for those leaving the earthly life and going to the spiritual and incorporeal world, it seems to me, have not understood the meaning of this life, but follow the common idea of the rabble, because that is how they have been accustomed to love the present life, no matter what kind it is."

(Gregory of Nyssa, *To the Mourners, for Those Who Have Gone From the Present Life to the Eternal*).

CHAPTER ONE

The Other World

In a previous chapter of the present study, we accepted as a given, as an undoubted fact, that at death the soul, the spiritual being of man, is separated from his fleshly, earthly life. And the body returns "to the ground from out of it you were taken" (Genesis 3.19), and it disintegrates into the original elements from which it was composed, while the soul remains eternally immortal.

This is a basic and unalterable doctrine of faith of our Orthodox Christian Church. But immediately the question arises:

"What happens then to the soul? What kind of spiritual being remains? Will the soul acquire another body perhaps, ethereal, but which will occupy a small or large concrete and tangible space in the other world beyond? And what kind of a world perchance is that world, and what is the place of our soul and its future in that world beyond?"

For these natural as well as devout questions, we will consult the Holy Scriptures and, combining related verses, we will endeavor to draw out the conclusions which, as much as possible, might satisfy the desire of devout persons.

In many places of the Holy Scriptures, we have the explicit assurance of our Savior Christ that he shall come a second time to this world, but then as a Judge of the universe. This is called the *Parousia* or "Second Coming." In the Gospel according to Saint Matthew, our Savior Jesus Christ himself says:

> When the Son of man comes in his glory, and all the angels with him, then he will sit on the glorious throne. Before him will be gathered all the nations, and he will separate them one from another as a shepherd separates the sheep from the goats, and he will place the sheep

The Other World

at his right hand, but the goats at the left. Then the King will say to those at the right hand: "Come, O blessed of my Father, inherit the Kingdom prepared for you from the foundation of the world . . . " Then he will say to those at his left hand, "Depart from me, you cursed, into the eternal fire prepared for the devil and his angels . . . " (Matthew 25.31-34, 41).

From this Gospel reading, we have two different, but definite, teachings:
 a. that the Son of God will come again, but as a judge, and
 b. that a General Judgment of all the human beings will take place.
This is a doctrine of faith. Our Church recites these teachings in abbreviated form in the *Symbol of Faith,* i.e., in the Creed, the *"Pistevo,"* as we call it and which was formulated by the first two Ecumenical Councils:

> And he shall come again in glory to judge the living and the dead, and of his Kingdom there shall be no end.

At this General Judgment during the Second Coming (*Parousia*) of Christ, all human beings will appear physically. Each soul, i.e., will appear in its body to be rewarded with it or to be punished with it. From the many verses in the Holy Scriptures which assure us of this, we offer the following as sufficient from the Second Epistle of Saint Paul to the Corinthians:

> For we must all appear before the judgment seat of Christ so that each one may receive good or evil according to what he has done in the body (2 Corinthians 5.10).

Concerning which body will be resurrected at the Second Coming, we shall deal with in another place later. Here, this is all that we are saying in order that we may state that from the day of the death of a person until the Second Coming, whose time is unkown even to the angels, the soul will exist without a body. Nowhere in the Holy Scriptures is it mentioned that the soul during this time will have a body.

Even though after death until the Second Coming of the Lord and the Final Judgment the souls will have no body, they will be bodiless, immaterial spirits, Holy Scripture teaches us that they will be in some place, in a definite space. In the Gospel according to Saint Luke, in the "Parable of the Unmerciful Rich Man and Poor Lazaros," we are given the information that there is a definite place in which the souls exist.

In this Parable, the soul of the rich man which was in Hades, being in torment, "saw Abraham far off and Lazaros in his bosom" (Luke 16.23). That phrase, "far off," indicates a place, an expanse of space. Also, when the soul of the rich man asked Abraham to "send Lazaros to dip the end of his finger in water and cool his tongue" (Luke 16.24), he answers: "And besides this, between us and you a great chasm has been fixed in order that those who would pass from here to you may not be able, and none may cross from there to us" (Luke 16:26).

Therefore, the bodiless souls from death until the Second Coming exist in some definite place.[7]

But what is that place? We shall deal with this is the following chapter.

CHAPTER TWO

Hades: The Place and Life of the Souls

The New Testament calls the place to which the souls go and remain after death until the Second Coming, Hades. At times, the New Testament with the word, "Hades," characterizes separately the place where the sinful souls are punished. But this is not always the case. Generally, Hades, as is mentioned in many parts of the New Testament, is the same for the good and the evil souls, but it is divided into two parts. The one is called, "Place of Comfort," the other, "Place of Torment." The Place of Comfort is the place where the souls of the good and devout go. The Place of Torment is the place where the souls of the evil and impious are held.

The New Testament contains other names with which the holy authors describe these two places. The Place of Comfort is also called: "the bosom of Abraham," "Heaven," "third Heaven," "heavenly Jerusalem," and "Kingdom of Heaven." The Place of Torment is also referred to as "prison," "Hades," etc.

Therefore, the souls exist after death in these two places, but also in different qualitative conditions until the Second Coming of the Lord, i.e., in the Place of Comfort or in the Place of Torment.

From all this, it is obvious and logical that the selection of the good and the evil, and the place of separation of the one from the other, should have some purpose. And it is impossible that this purpose should not look forward to the reward of the good and the punishment of the evil souls.

This is the purpose and the teaching of the "Parable of the Unmerciful Rich Man and Poor Lazaros" (Luke 16.19-31). When the unmerciful rich man, being in torment, cried out to Abraham and said, "Send Lazaros to dip the end of his finger in water and cool my tongue," Abraham answered: "Son, according to the quality of the life of each of you on earth, you are repaid now: he is comforted here (consoled, rewarded), and you are in anguish (punished).

However, the kind and amount of reward for the good souls in Hades, as well as the kind and amount of punishment for the evil souls is temporary. The full reward or punishment will be given to the good and evil souls at the Second Coming of Christ. Because then the Final Judgment shall take place, and the Book of Life of each person will be opened and their deeds shall be examined and audited.

During this transient period of centuries until the Second Coming, the good souls will enjoy only a part of the happiness which they will receive at the Last Judgment Day. And, in like manner, the evil souls will be punished by only a part of the punishment which they deserve and which they will fully receive after the Last Judgment Day.

The Self-Consciousness of the Soul in Hades

But, however small or great the partial reward or punishment of the souls in Hades may be until the Second Coming, in order for them to feel the happiness or the punishment, it is indeed necessary for them to know why they are being rewarded or punished. Otherwise, this reward or punishment would not make any sense. However, for the souls to know why they are being rewarded or why they are being punished, they must remember their deeds which they did during their life on earth. And, furthermore, since they will remember their deeds, it is impossible that they not remember the persons or the groups with which they were, in one way or another, related with those deeds, i.e., the souls will remember those persons which they benefited or harmed in their life on earth. And since they will remember those persons, they will certainly also remember the circumstances under which they performed the good or bad deeds and the time when these occurred here on earth. For example, a person's soul is punished in Hades because during his life on earth, he committed a murder or a robbery. In order for his soul to feel the punishment, it must have the memory of its crime which was committed on earth. And having the memory of its crime in Hades, it must also retain there the thought that it was evil, i.e., it must be conscious of this unlawful act. And, again, in order to retain the memory of the crime and be conscious of it as an evil. And, for this reason, it is punished, certainly, it must also remember the instances in which the crime was committed, and the person who was murdered, and the objects that were stolen as well as where and when all these things occurred.

But the totality of a person's acts, together with the remembrances of the place and time that they occurred and the different circumstances in which they were done (good or evil, regardless), all this totality comprises the life of a person here on earth — his existence. Because what else is the life of a person here on earth other than the totality of his deeds, his thoughts, his spoken words, his ambitions, and his feelings?

And when a person admits that he did these things, i.e., that the totality of his deeds comprise his life, and not that of someone else, this is called the self-consciousness of an individual. And when the soul of a person in Hades continues to have knowledge of all these things which comprised his life on earth, his being, and admits this is the same, and not another existence of, the person that did all these things, then we say that the soul retains its self-consciousness in Hades.

This matter of self-consciousness of the soul in Hades is of great significance, because on this is based whether death is truly such a sad event as our hearts usually characterize it, being wounded by our separation from loved ones by death.

Communication of the Souls with the Living

We, finally, have reached the syllogistic conclusion which is also the teaching of Holy Scripture, that each soul in Hades (regardless if it is in Paradise or in the Place of Torment) has self-consciousness and remembers persons, things, and events of the earthly life.

But from this, again, it is obvious that the soul will be

aware of these persons, things, and events which continue to exist and happen even after that soul, by death, left this world and went to the other life beyond the grave. And this, that is, that the soul in Hades is aware of persons and events which occur in this world, must be much greater for the soul in Hades with those with whom it was related: relatives, friends, co-workers, etc., when it was physically on earth.

These memories of the soul's relations with relatives and friends and co-workers will be stronger, and the feeling of love towards them deeper and of longer duration, and the desire to communicate with them more nostalgic.

And, since the soul in Hades is aware of persons and conditions that exist on earth, it is natural for us to agree that, by the same token, the soul is concerned about them. This is not merely a conclusion resulting from a series of syllogisms which we made in this and the previous chapter. It is a fact which Holy Scripture teaches. In the Book of Revelation, it is stated that:

> the souls of the martyrs cry out against the persecutions by the idolaters which continue to plague the Christians on earth, and ask the Lord Christ, "O Sovereign Lord, avenge our blood on those who dwell upon the earth" (Revelation 6.9).

In the Parable of the Unmerciful Rich Man, he, finding himself in the Place of Torment, expresses his deep concern and filial sentiments towards his brothers who were still alive, and begs Abraham to send Lazaros to them to assure them concerning the torment which awaits them, in order that they might repent before it is too late. The verse from the Gospel is very clear:

> And he (the soul of the rich man addressing Abraham) said, "Then I beg you, father, to send him (Lazaros) to my father's house, for I have five brothers, so that he may warn them, lest they also come into this place of torment" (Luke 16.27).

Hades: The Place and Life of the Souls

The concern, therefore, of that soul in Hades for his brothers is assured indisputably by our Savior Jesus Christ who related this Parable. This provides us with the teaching that the souls of our beloved persons which have died are aware of our life and are concerned for it. And, of course, this is a great consolation in the case of death which offers a balm of comfort to our hearts when pained by the death of a loved one.

In this manner, the death of a loved one appears as nothing more than a trip to a far and foreign country, where he retains a warm love for us and a never-ending concern for everything related to our lives. And we have the hope that, someday, he will tire of that foreign country and return to be with us again. Or we wait for him to send us a letter inviting us to go where they are, so that we may all live happily together. But since the first instance, i.e., for them to return home to us, is out of the question, and for sure the second instance will come to pass, and, indeed, without the letter of invitation because all of us, without exception, sooner or later, will die some day, the following question arises: "Why is there such a terror of death which, without examination, we consider as horrendous and sinister?"

CHAPTER THREE

Necessary Summary of Questions about the Preceding

Up to this point, we have reached the following conclusions based on the witness of the Holy Scriptures, which are also the teachings of our Orthodox Church:

1. that after the death of the body, the soul goes to Hades. If our deeds in life were according to God's will, the soul will go to the Place of Comfort or Paradise. If our deeds were evil, then the soul will go to the Place of Torment or Damnation.
2. that in these places, i.e., in Hades, the souls will not remain forever. They shall only remain there until the Second Coming (Parousia) of the Son of God and the resurrection of the dead.
3. that in these places in which the souls are rewarded or punished, neither the reward nor the punishment will be fully given. The full reward or punishment will be given to the souls after the resurrection of the dead at the Last Judgment Day. In the meantime, the souls will have only partial happiness or adversity, which shall be given fully after the Second Coming of the Lord.
4. that the souls, even with this partial reward or partial punishment, will know the reason why each is given. They will know that they are being rewarded for specific good deeds, or punished for specific evil deeds, and they shall remember these deeds and the persons and events with which they were related.
5. that since the souls remember all these and know that they themselves did them as persons in life, without

any doubt whatsoever, the souls will retain self-consciousness in Hades.

6. that having self-consciousness and remembering the persons and conditions which continue to exist on earth, and especially remembering their relatives, the souls are concerned about them and continue to love them and desire to communicate with them.

From all the above, now another conclusion comes to the fore which is very significant for this matter of death, the following:

Since, after death, the soul watches with concern over the dear ones who remain alive in this world, it is natural and logical to conclude that it also is aware of and is concerned about the souls of persons who were dear to it on earth but who died and went to Hades before it, or even after it went there. In other words, it is obvious from the above that there is communication among the souls of the dead with each other.

This conclusion is based on the sweet consolation of every person whose heart has been wounded by the death of a loved one. The contrite mother and the deeply wounded father say to their dead child who, like an angel dressed in pure white clothing, is lying in a casket before them: "I will soon come with you where you are going. Wait for me; we will meet you very soon." A faithful wife says to her beloved spouse who, like a shadow slipped away from her in an untimely death and went to the world beyond the grave: "My life was your life, and my soul shall again be yours. We will meet there where nothing will ever separate us again."

The loving children say to a mother or father whose lifeless body lies on the deathbed speechless, without a response to those mournful cries: "You left us orphans in the stormy sea of this life and you have gone. But some day, sooner or later, we will come to meet you there."

All these serve as a miraculous balm of comfort to the

hearts that are deeply and sincerely hurt. They are words of an inner faith, the breath of the voice of the Infinite God Who, deep in our sinful souls, in times of severe testing, consents lovingly and whispers unknown truths, revelations, and mysterious realities which are, at the same time, wholesomely strengthening our much troubled human existence.

However, even though this assurance that there is communication of the souls of loved ones who passed away in an untimely death with us, and, further, that there is communication of their souls with our souls in the other world beyond, it is also a great balm of comfort which makes death appear no more as something terrible but like a minor event in our entire existence. Yet, an unanswered but very justifiable question still remains, the following:

"Sure, our souls will communicate with each other in Hades when we all go there. But why does God take from our bosom loved ones in an untimely death and literally break our hearts?"

This question will be answered in the following chapter.

CHAPTER FOUR

Is Untimely Death an Injustice?

In a previous chapter, we concluded that an untimely death, if it does not deprive a person of the aesthetic, intellectual, and sentimental pleasures, i.e., if the soul in Hades has such pleasures, and even more and better pleasures, then the soul is not wronged because, in this case, the person loses nothing by an untimely death. But, again, the question arises: Even if a person does not lose anything in an untimely death, why doesn't God protect a person so that he would not die in his youth, and indeed in childhood before he grows old, and not wound the hearts of his loved ones?"

The answer to this question has need of the following premise:

Do we believe in divine Providence? Divine Providence is a doctrine of our Orthodox faith. It is an inviolable teaching of our Church that God, the Creator of the universe, is its Governor. He provides and sustains the world and directs it to its final purpose. The same is taught by the Church concerning man, i.e., that God provides for man and, indeed, especially for him. For this reason, the Holy Scriptures require that we ask for God's help along the entire road of our life. And this is also the purpose of prayer when it is not only to glorify God.

The Apostle Peter in his First Epistle says:

Cast all your anxieties on him, for he cares for you (1 Peter 5.7).

In the Gospel according to Saint Matthew, we read:

Are not two sparrows sold for a penny? And not one of them will fall to the ground without your Father's will. But even the hairs of your head are all numbered. Fear not, therefore; you are of more value than many sparrows (Matthew 10.29-31).

This should be enough, I imagine, to prove that everything that happens in the lives of humans happens for some purpose of divine Providence. And since it happens by the will of divine Providence, this purpose assuredly must be for the good of the person for whom they are done because divine Provience never intends to do evil.

Certainly this good is not always limited only to the life of a person on earth; it also concerns the life of the soul, and especially for the soul, as was emphasized in my previous book. Divine Providence tests the earthly life of persons for their benefit. The greater that the good is for the soul which divine Providence aims, so much greater the trial can be. Indeed, such a trial could reach the point of death, either of the person for whose soul divine Providence is working, or of another person whose death might possibly serve the life of the souls of others.

And since we have set down this teaching of our Church as a precept, let us return now to the question: "Why does God allow the untimely death in the early life of a person?" And now the answer is: "With an untimely death, divine Providence looks to the good of the life of the soul of such a person, or to the life of the souls of those persons who are dear to him."

Having in mind this answer, let us examine a few such instances. And first: If we examine the pain which is caused by the wounding of the heart by the untimely death of a loved one, we shall find that it cannot be supported by any true justification. It is a pain that results more from an uncensured feeling. It might even be based on instinct, paternal, maternal, filial, erotic, friendly, etc. Experience, however, and history of social life prove to us that the feeling of love, affection for relatives or for friends, because of which hearts are wounded by the demise of a loved one, is a transient feeling, very dubious, and is often merely conventional.

Is Untimely Death an Injustice? 51

Two or three examples will help us to understand this more clearly:

The most pure and holy feeling of love is that of parents for their children, especially that of the mother. The strongest feeling of love, however, and at times indomitable, is the feeling of love of a person for one of the opposite sex, which is called *eros*.

For this reason, we begin with this, examining it to see if deep pain is justified by the separation that untimely death causes.

When a young man and a young woman love each other chastely, but strongly, and it happens that one of the two gets sick, or an accident occurs and one dies, this untimely death leaves a deep trauma in the heart of the one that continues to live. Those who know the details and the deep love of these two persons, judging the situation in an unstudied manner, raise questions and ask: "Why did God do such an injustice to separate that loving couple by taking one of them?"

But in view of this thought, let all those who can spare an hour or so sometime become judges to examine the various social phenomena. How often has it happened that persons insanely in love with each other, who before they married lived with the breath of the other and denied parents, brothers, sisters, and relatives and even disregarded social conditions and eloped because they imagined that it would be absolutely impossible for the one to live without the other? And then, after a while, maybe five or six months later, or even one or two years later, they began to bitterly hate each other, and their life together deteriorated literally into a living hell, and they considered divorce as their only salvation in order to prevent a possible crime, a cruel murder or poisoning or any other harm of one from the other, where before they were the most adorable person in all the world? And having the experience of such frequently occurring examples, we ask: "When we daily see so many other couples in society separating by such circumstances, what can assure us that the persons who were separated by an untimely death of the one, would not have come to the same point of hate?" Because they loved one another so strongly and sincerely before marriage, what assurance do we have that they would continue to be united in love for the rest of their lives? And why, then, should we consider it a terrible misfortune and injustice if death sometimes untimely separates two persons who love each other, taking one and leaving the other with the sweetest memories that remain vividly alive and are unforgettable? And if it were possible for one to look into the crystal ball of the magician fortune-teller and see the future of a couple like that and see the condition of hate into which later their great love would deteriorate, would one not prefer and seek with all one's heart the death of one of them? In this instance, at least, the hope would remain that the desire of their meeting would be realized in the other world and they would then live forever together in the life beyond, where there is no fear anymore that love will change into satiety and into hate.

And that which is surely true in the case of love before marriage, or in a marriage itself, wouldn't it be similarly true in every other kind of love whose bonds are broken untimely, but perhaps charitably very often, by Charon?

And what is different in the complex and unstable relationships in the life of society and individuals that loved each other, where lovers or engaged couples or spouses, or father or mother for son and daughter, or brothers and sisters or any other relative, that the separation by death be considered a terrible misfortune? Don't we daily have innumerable examples of uncontrollable enmity between brothers and sisters and even hate of parents for their children, and married or single children for their parents? And don't we have a great number of patricides, infanticides, and fraticides, and murders in general, as the result of hate against other persons who previously were united by loving tenderness, invincible love, blind adoration; can anyone say?

And who knows the future, to be sure, in one or another untimely death of a loved one, that none of the above examples would not have happened if untimely death had not charitably come? And if either, as some might say, it was so written or it was the result of a sick mind, two persons who loved each other came to such a bitter hate who would not have preferred and hoped with all his heart for death as a benevolent provider, instead of such a terrible thing to happen which is worse than eternal separation in the life beyond the grave?

CHAPTER FIVE

Are There Pleasures in the World Beyond Similar to Those of this World?

I have devoted two chapters of this study to explain the spiritual, intellectual, sentimental, and aesthetic pleasures that a person has in life. And I emphasized that such pleasures make life worth living and, furthermore, that they improve the life of the soul.

However, I projected this question: "Since there are pleasures in life, whatever they may be, is not an untimely death a cruel thing which deprives a person of such pleasure by taking him before he had a chance to fully enjoy them?"

And I answered that it certainly would be cruel if, in dying an untimely death, a person himself, his soul, his being, would be deprived of those pleasures forever. But if, in the life beyond the grave, such pleasures do exist and, indeed, livelier, greater, and more beautifully expressed for the soul, then we could say that it would be absolutely unjustified for a Christian to be saddened if he should die, even in an untimely death.

Therefore, the question now is stated as follows:

a. "Do there exist in the life beyond the grave more and and better spiritual, intellectual, sentimental, and aesthetic pleasures than those that a devout being has here on earth, or at least equal to them?" and

b. "If they do exist, does the soul there feel them and enjoy them, so that we can say that a person dying an untimely death is not cheated by their interruption?"

Before we answer these two questions, we must separate the souls of the devout that are in the Place of Comfort or Paradise from the souls that are in the Place of Torment or Damnation. And when we separate them, we shall examine these questions in regards, first, to the good souls, and then in regards to the condemned souls. And, thus, we will

Are There Pleasures in the World Beyond?

have the answer immediately, if we remember:
  a. that the souls in Hades have self-consciousness and that they are rewarded for their good deeds done while alive, i.e., they shall receive retribution.

And since the souls beyond the grave have self-consciousness and remember their deeds in life, the persons, things, and conditions, and feel the joy in reminiscing about them, it is inevitably natural to believe that in Hades the souls retain all the attributes which made it possible for them to feel, especially the good and beautiful in their life on earth.

And since the soul is able to have these feelings, it also has the impressions which caused it to be happy, i.e., to have spiritual, intellectual, sentiemental, and aesthetic pleasures. And especially since it knows that for most of these pleasures which it had in life it will also be rewarded with them after death. We must further agree that the soul in the afterlife has these pleasures stronger, livelier, more beautifully, and longer lasting than it had them in life. And, again, this is natural because it is now liberated and free from the physical body whose weaknesses and limitations, together with the material and physical demands of the body impinge upon these beautiful and pure impressions and distort them.

But now let us come to more concrete situations and examine each group of these beautiful and saving pleasures separately.

1. *Spiritual pleasures,* that is, the satisfaction of the soul of a devout person which he has in his earthly life because of his faith and devotion toward God and his only-begotten Son, our Savior, Jesus Christ, and communion with him.

We know that many people find such spiritual pleasures in their physical life, even though they are surrounded every hour by sin and they struggle to avoid being slaves to it. But this struggle often is such that even the most devout person comes forth spiritually weakened and, indeed, with some small dents in his steel-clad devotion. And even though he still enjoys these spiritual pleasures, yet he is tyrannized by the torment of doubt that slyly comes to mind secretly in difficult times and says that perhaps faith is nothing more than the belief in non-existence and is laboring in vain. Such doubt becomes very persistent and weakens markedly the moral resistance of a person against sin.

And since in view of all this a person in this life has spiritual pleasures, his soul will have these pleasures much more in the life beyond the grave in the world beyond because: There the soul, undisturbed by the pleasures of the material needs of the physical body, free from intellectual distortions and faulty doubts, and far from anything that might darken the way to the superior and true, it will feel incomparably greater, more vividly, more beautifully, more satisfyingly, the inexpressible pleasure of communion with God. It will feel incomparable joy and supreme satisfaction that the faith it had on earth was not a delusion or an absurdity, but it was a faith in the True Being, a faith in absolute Truth, a faith that was a special gift to its being by the Supreme Being.

Such spiritual pleasures that a devout soul experiences in Hades, more real, more beautiful, more satisfying, and longer lasting than all that its being had in the perishable life on earth not only makes death not a matter of sorrow, but beneficial.

2. *Intellectual pleasures* are the beautiful impressions that satisfy the intellectual desires of the soul of a person. It is not necessary for a devout person to have intellectual pleasures in his life here on earth. A devout person can exist without experiencing all the intellectual pleasures that I mentioned in a previous chapter, without suffering the least substantive harm to his soul.

But a devout person can very well experience the most beautiful impressions and the sweetest satisfaction that comes from intellectual pleasures. Such were, for example, the great Fathers of the Church, Origen, Gregory of Nyssa, Augustine, etc., as well as the great philosophers and scientists who were Christians, such as Leibnitz, Pascal, Newton, Flammarion, Pasteur, and infinitely more of lesser scientific

Are There Pleasures in the World Beyond? 57

worth or, in general, intellectuals.

And now the question arises: "Will the souls in Hades experience such pleasures there? Will any devout soul whose life on earth found such satisfaction and joy in these pleasures, be deprived of them by untimely or natural death?"

The Holy Scriptures do not assure us literally in this matter. But the series of syllogisms is so unbroken that they lead us to this conclusion and to this conviction, so that we are justified in saying that the Scriptures verify this, albeit indirectly. And for this reason: The abilities of the mind, which all together are called the intellect of man, are a gift from God, and are the "Ten Talents" which as Christ says in the "Parable of the Ten Talents" (Matthew 25.14-30), a Master gave to his servant. The devout intellectual cultivates the "ten talents" by his work and his devotion to letters, science, the arts, discoveries, inventions. Our Lord said that when the time came for the Master to settle accounts with his servants, he found that the servant to whom he had given five talents had made good use of them. He had doubled them and made them ten talents. The Master not only gave him the ten talents to keep, but he also gave him the one talent that he had given to the wicked and slothful servant who had hidden it in the ground.[9]

The day on which the Master in the parable came to settle accounts with his servants obviously refers to the Final Judgment Day of the Second Coming (*Parousia*) of Christ.

However, as proved in a previous chapter, the devout persons will receive only a part of this reward immediately after the death of the body, i.e., in Hades, in the Place of Comfort, during the Intermediate State of souls, just as the evil persons will receive partial punishment there.

Therefore, together with the other rewards which he will receive in the life beyond the grave, the soul of a devout intellectual shall also receive the reward of intellectual pleasures which he enjoyed in his earthly life and which gave him such pleasurable satisfaction. But he will have more enjoyment there because, as Christ said, he shall receive at the Final Judgment that which was not used by the wicked and slothful servant. And even in the Intermediate State, again he shall have part of this unused "Talent."

Consequently, I further believe that beyond the grave these intellectual pleasures of the soul of a devout intellectual shall not only be more, but also more beautiful and more satisfying for the present spiritual being of a person. Then again, the soul during its occupation with these intellectual pleasures beyond the grave, and since it will be without the limiting material physical problem, i.e., the body, will now have its intellectual power free, a rested mind surrounded by a most transparent intellectual atmosphere.

Thus, quietly, it will come and enjoy without interruption, more satisfyingly, the great infinite problems of the universe from which only one small particle(and that dark and confusing), the scientific problems of the earth and of human existence that are known on earth. Standing before the solutions of these, the human mind is dazzled in amazement.

With all this, we arrive at the inevitable conclusion that besides the spiritual pleasures that the soul experiences in the world beyond, it also experiences intellectual pleasures which are greater and more satisfying than those that are experienced here on earth.

3. *Sentimental pleasures,* that is, spiritual satisfaction from the noble statements of the soul which are the result of love for neighbor, and for every other human being.

In the chapter that I had devoted to these, I mentioned the philadelphic deeds of man which gave him sentimental pleasure. Such deeds are: the forgiving of those who harmed us, charity, the visitation of and consoling the sick and imprisoned, defending those who were wronged, fearless witnessing in favor of those falsely slandered, self-denial for every noble idea, love of parents for their children, love and obedience of children for their parents and of spouses towards each other, sincere friendships, etc. And again, the same persistent question arises whose true answer minimizes the fear of death — the following:

"Since the practice of these good deeds result in sentimental pleasures for the devout person and satisfy a spiritual need and make his life worth living, will his soul also have such sentimental pleasures in his life beyond the grave so that in the life beyond he will not be deprived of those pleasures which he had in life and not consider death, whether untimely or natural, as an injustice?"

For the answer to this question, we must separate those sentimental deeds into two categories. In the first category, we will include those deeds for which there are simply no reasons in the life beyond the grave to cause them. The second category will include those deeds which are caused by sentimental needs that also exist in the life beyond.

For example, charity, visiting and consoling the sick and the imprisoned, defending those wronged, the fearless witness in favor of falsely slandered persons, etc. are impossible to be practiced in the world beyond because there are neither poor nor imprisoned, nor sick, nor unjustly wronged or slandered, nor others in any other manner unjustly suffering that exist there. And since the devout and virtuous person practiced these virtues in life because he felt sorrow in his soul for the travail of those who so suffered, the sentimental pleasure that he received when he helped these unfortunate ones was more negative, without satisfaction. On the other hand, such a pleasure was not necessary for the happiness either for his soul, nor for his life on earth. On the contrary, indeed, the heart of a philanthropist desires that there were no unfortunate persons in the world, even though he might not have ever had the sentimental pleasure of benefitting those suffering and unfortunate persons. Therefore, even though the soul will not have in the life beyond the grave such pleasures, not only does untimely death not deprive anything from a person but, further, it has some positive pleasures that it lives, henceforth, in a world in which misfortune has no part.

4. *The Rest of the sentimental pleasures*, are those which are derived from the love of parents for children and children for parents, spouses' love for each other, and love among brothers and sisters and friends. But who can surmise that such sentimental pleasures and pure satisfaction of such

pleasures will not be had by souls in the world beyond, which are rewarded there as devout and virtuous. And who would imagine, even if he could, that Christ, who rewards every good, would deprive the devout in the world beyond such pure Christian pleasures which he enjoyed in his life on earth?

Our Savior, Jesus Christ, in his Parable of the Unmerciful Rich Man and Poor Lazaros, speaks of the soul of the rich man in Hades as retaining feelings of tender concern and love for his living brothers. But then, can we agree that such a gift, such a privilege, which God gives even to unworthy souls condemned to the Place of Torment, would be deprived from the devout souls which he himself placed in the Place of Comfort and rewards accordingly so that they would be happy?

And I am sure that there is no doubt that not only does the soul have such sentimental pleasures in the world beyond, but it enjoys them more satisfactorily, more purely, more beautifully. Because no matter how ethereal the mutual love of parents and children, of spouses or brothers and sisters become here on earth, there always are so many daily avalanches of collisions between persons that love one another when one word, glance, one motion might be able somehow, at some time, to strain the warmth of love they have between them.[10]

While in the world beyond, any such thing is excluded and the horizon of pure sentimental love remains unclouded, rosy, and infinite. And not only for the persons who loved each other in their life on earth, but also for many others with whom they had a beautiful noble friendly relation, even though remote.

5. *Aesthetic pleasures,* that is, the exhilaration of the soul by the beauties of nature, the universe, and technical and artistic works that are produced by humans of outstanding abilities who are endowed by God the Creator.

I ask the reader to re-read the Chapter Two where I mention many such pleasures so that it will not be necessary to repeat them here. And then the following question arises: "Will the soul that had some artistic, poetic, musical, sculptural, architectural, mechanical, or other abilities on

Are There Pleasures in the World Beyond? 61

earth, from which pleasure was derived in its aesthetic exhilaration, have such pleasures in the life beyond?"

For the answer to this question, we shall find the assurance in two hypotheses:

a. if the soul will retain these abilities to assume and appreciate representations that are in the universe they will produce similar aesthetic pleasures in the life beyond, and,

b. whether such artistic representations exist in the life beyond.

As to the first, I believe that it is the same as what I said concerning the intellectual pleasures, i.e., just as the intellectual abilities are a gift from God and are included in the "ten talents" of the parable, in like manner, the ability of aesthetic artistic comprehension that some persons have is a privileged gift of God.

And since this, as well as the other, is a higher endowment to man by God, we cannot see why the same God who gave it would take it away in the world beyond, since that person's soul was devout in its earthly life and increased, or at least endeavored to increase, "the five talents and make them ten." Therefore, we believe that the soul of a devout person retains the abilities that he had in his earthly life as well in the world beyond in order to have aesthetic pleasures. Furthermore, these abilities (we can believe without being sure) are greatly developed in the life of the soul beyond the grave. And it is so, not only because there preceded a practice of these abilities of the soul in its earthly life, but also because the soul, completely undistracted by worldly cares, gives itself completely to pure aesthetic pleasures, if in the life beyond such artistic representations and compositions exist there. But do such representations and compositions exist in the life beyond? This is the second hypothesis that I had made with the "ifs" and must be proven. And here is the proof:

Since, in a previous chapter, we agreed that the soul retains its self-consciousness in Hades, communicates with the loved ones remaining on earth, and clearly remembers conditions, times, places, and incidents of its deeds on earth (which also continue after the death of its body) and is concerned about them, surely it will continue to be concerned about them in the world beyond. And the soul will continue to be aware of the beauties of nature with which its life in the world had much in common, and it will be aware of them not for a short or long time, but for as long as this earthly sphere and everything in it will continue to exist. And not only will the soul be aware of the artistic beauty, as it knew it when as a living person with a body it lived in the visible nature, but it will feel these beautiful representations and compositions better, more clearly, more deeply. And they produce the aesthetic pleasures which result from the idyllic and other natural scenes and harmonious compositions of which, with the weak eyes and rough drums of the organs of hearing of the human body, we become aware.

Certainly there are unimaginable harmonious representations in the universe, in the extensive and deep distance that we see in the chaos around us, which is resplendent with the myriads of stars that comprise the visible and unseen galaxies and even entire worlds. The soul, liberated from the limitations of physical eyes will enjoy their artistic beauty in the world beyond. There surely one will listen to harmonious musical compositions, just as today we listen to Beethoven's Sonatas, Chopin's Serenades, and the operas of Wagner, in comparison to the sounds in our ears of the primitive drum beating of the barbarian natives in the African jungles. They will be the harmonious compositions of angelic hymns, bands of children's melodies, the mystic, yet sweet-sounding, hymn of the entire universe to its Creator. The soul of a devout person, hearing all these, will vibrate with inexpressible aesthetic pleasure which even the most mystical and inpired maestro of musical harmony has never felt even for a thousandth of a second in this earthly world. Thus, we have arrived at the pleasant and true conclusion that the soul will have in the life beyond the spiritual, intellectual, sentimental, and aesthetic pleasures which alone are able to make the life of man on earth worth living.

Furthermore, the soul will have these pleasures in the

Are There Pleasures in the World Beyond? 63

life beyond more fully, more nobly, more beautifully, more satisfyingly. On the one hand, the causes that produce them and the conditions which they reflect on the soul that is being rewarded in Hades are in themselves magnificent because they belong to the infinite and perfect spiritual world. On the other hand, the soul in the world beyond is able to receive more and better impressions which give beautiful aesthetic pleasures, because the soul is a spirit there without a body. In earthly life the body, with its weaknesses and limitations, allows the soul to receive only limited and incomplete impressions from the external world as well as from its inner world. And, above all, in the world beyond the soul has the satisfaction that it is in direct contact with our Savior Jesus Christ from whom it has uninterrupted approval and relative reward. Such satisfaction cannot be exchanged or compared with anything else.

In that case, therefore, is death, even untimely death, cruel? Or is it a progressive step of the soul from one condition that is only tolerated on earth to another condition that is desirable — to the spiritual land of dreams and unending happiness?

PART FOUR

CHAPTER ONE

Rewards and Punishments in the Life Beyond the Grave

Up to this point we have dealt with matters related to the condition in which the soul of a devout and virtuous person exists in Hades. But all persons are not like these. There are impious and unmerciful and evil-doers in this world. And, indeed, let us not hide the truth, we confess that evil persons comprise by far the greater part of the human population on earth.

The Scripture writers assure us of this by calling the devout and virtuous persons the *elect*. The elect in every instance are always the few. What will happen then to the unworthy in the life beyond?

Holy Scripture literally says that they will be punished. And the place and kind of their punishment is designated by different names: i.e., "Place of Torment," "prison," "Gehenna of fire," "the Outer darkness where men will weep and gnash their teeth," etc.

But from the early years of Christianity until today, the question constantly arises: Must we construe these punishments as literally true? And if we accept them as such, how can a soul that is spirit be punished by them, no matter how evil it is?

The answer to this question has been different during the various Christian centuries and as given by the various Fathers of the Church and ecclesiastical writers.

There are those who claimed that the punishment of the impious and evil persons would literally be of fire, fire, and more fire; fiery rivers, lakes of fire, boiling pots, and anything similar or worse. Their books and sermons were permeated with an unquenchable thirst to see sinners being tyrannized horribly, something irreconcilable to Christianity, the representatives of love. In short, their imagination devised horrible materialistic torments for the impious.[11]

However, there were many other writers who looked at this matter very humanely, more conciliatorily. Of these, some sought to present hell as a temporary cleansing in which the soul would remain for a period of time and be purged of its sins (purgatory). And from there it would go to Paradise. Others considered hell to be eternal sleep (nihilism). But the conciliatory opinions concerning the souls of the impious after death should, if they are not based completely on the explicit teachings of Holy Scripture, at least not be contrary to the spirit and the basic teachings of Holy Scripture.

a. Only the Christian life on earth leads to the Kingdom of God, and

b. that each according to his works shall be glorified or shamed.

It would be great for each of us, who by our own deeds are drowning in sin, if there existed a "purgatory," in which the damned souls could be cleansed from sin and then proceed as saved into Paradise. And it would be even greater yet, perhaps, for souls after physical death to fall into an eternal sleep, or even not to be born at all. But whatever may seem great to us does not mean that that is the teaching of the Christian faith. Neither is it proper for us to create doctrines which the Holy Scriptures do not approve of and which do not in any manner whatsoever by their liberalism contribute to the establishment of the Kingdom of God on earth, which Christ taught that we should always seek.

Avoiding, therefore, the extremes, we should discern the punishment of the damned somewhere between the unimaginable cruelty of materialistic fire and the ideas produced by liberalism. The latter negates all moral laws here on earth with the ulterior motive that we will be forgiven and everything will be corrected in the world beyond. Or that the one dreamless eternal sleep, nihilism, will equalize every iniquity later.

In order for us to mention what kind of penalties there will be for those condemned to hell, it is absolutely necessary first to see which are the rewards for the souls of the devout in Paradise.

It is true that the Holy Scriptures do not clearly define what kind of rewards the just and devout shall receive in the world beyond. They are merely called in general: "Paradise," "bosom of Abraham," "the throne of God and of the Lamb," "Communion with Patriarchs, or with the Saints or with the Holy Angels," "Kingdom of God," "Kingdom of Christ," "Kingdom of Heaven," "Reign of Christ," "Seeing God," etc. But these general titles of the Place of Comfort, just as the general titles for the Place of Torment which were mentioned previously, are not sufficiently enlightening. They merely indicate that in the one place, there is unutterable happiness, and in the other, terrible torment. In other words, two extremely different places. The descriptions of the New Testament of the Kingdom of Heaven, of the New Jerusalem, and the Place of Torment have the same characteristics.

The vision of St. John in the Book of Revelation describes the Place of Beautitude as a city with golden streets and pearly gates, walls of jasper, sapphire, agate, emerald, onyx, carnelian, chrysolite, beryl, topaz, chrysoprase, jacinth, amethyst, and whatever other precious material the inspired writer saw in his spiritual ecstasy as his soul was engrossed in wonder before the heavenly vision. Consequently, he did not know how else to describe its magnificence except to describe it in a most materialistic way (see Revelation 21.11-25).

No Christian, regardless of how materialistic he may be, can agree that the Place of Comfort, the Kingdom of Heaven is a city whose walls have length in each one of its four sides of twelve thousand stadia all of jewels. Because, first of all, what value can gold, diamonds, pearls, etc. have for the soul which is a spirit?

We can say the same about the description of the Place of Torment, Hell. It is described as "Outer darkness," "Lake of fire," "place where the worm does not die," and "the place of weeping and the gnashing of teeth." But it is apparent also that despite these descriptive expressions, which describe as much as possible the horrendous punishment of a sinner, the real penalties must be of another kind.

Then again, it is certain that neither all the good and devout persons are of the same moral and religious quality. Nor do all the sinners deserve the same condemnation. There are degrees of devoutness. For example, any devout and moral tradesman today who is a believer and endeavors not to cheat anyone directly may give up to half of his profits for philanthropical causes. Notwithstanding all this, however, he does clear from his merchandise more than what he needs to live frugally, but we cannot say that, therefore, he will go to the Place of Torment. In any event, he cannot be in the same degree of blessedness as, for example, St. Basil is, who sold all that he had and, together with the income from his diocese, disposed of it all for those who were suffering. Moreover, his soul was continually turned towards the Divine, and he did not satisfy any desire of his body.

Between these two extreme qualities of life there are innumerable degrees of life in which thousands can be placed. Therefore, blessedness in the Place of Comfort is like an infinite ladder with innumerable steps, and naturally the rewards are proportionally given in an infinite number of ways.

Our Lord and Savior Jesus Christ assures us of this, not only with his phrase: "In my Father's house are many rooms" (John 14.2), but also with his assurance that "he will repay every man for what he has done" (Matthew 16.27).

We are obliged to say the same concerning the Place of Torment in which, again, there shall be different and infinite degrees of punishment. In the Gospel of St. Luke, we read:

> And that servant who knew his master's will, but did not make ready or act according to his will, shall receive a severe beating. But he who did not know, and did what deserved a beating, shall receive a light beating (Luke 12.47-48).

In other words, he who did not know the evil that he did will be punished less than one who knowingly committed evil.

In the Gospel according to St. Matthew, we also read:

> Truly, I say to you, it shall be more tolerable on the day of Judgment for the land of Sodom and Gomorrah than for that town (Matthew 10.15).

Here our Lord is referring to any town that would not receive the Apostles or listen to their words, i.e., that did not accept Christianity.

I mentioned these two Gospel passages to prove with the comparisons they make that there are degrees of punishment in the Place of Torment and, consequently, that the horrendous expressions: "Lake of fire, "the gnashing of teeth," "the worm that does not die," etc. are allegorical expressions that do not represent the reality of the penalties that are for the infinite degrees of the condemned souls.

Thus, we come to accept that in Paradise there will be an innumerable series of degrees of blessedness, from the highest degree of Saints which shall be near the Throne of God, to the lowest step, where those whose proportionate good and philanthropic deeds were such that they were not considered by God to be deserving of punishment.

And in Hell again there will be an innumerable series of degrees from the highest step where those will be whom God considered deserving of punishment to the lowest step where those will be who are calloused sinners who knowingly perpetrated evil and who are the most damned.

Chaos separates the highest step in the ladder of the condemned, the Place of Torment, from the lowest step in the ladder of Blessedness, Paradise, where the blessed will be, that is, the Place of Beatitude from the Place of Condemnation. The weak human mind is not able to define the place exactly where the line of separation is which separates the two places. Only inferentially will we be able to describe them in the next chapter.

Leaving the matter of penalties for another chapter, we only say here that that which decides the amount and quality of blessedness for a devout soul in the world beyond will be a double cause:

   a) the source from which blessedness will be given and

   b) the place which the soul will have in the endless series of beatitudinal degrees. Because on that again depends how much power the soul will have in receiving more or less blessings from the Divine Source.

CHAPTER TWO

The Source of Beatitude or Blessedness

This same attribute, the "Source of Beatitude," shows us that it can be no other than God himself. From him comes everything that is good, pleasing, satisfying, and all these in perfection. And if all persons in the life on earth do not have from God the good, the pleasing, and the satisfying, this does not mean that the Source is drying up and, as a result, has more for some and less for others, but rather because everyone does not endeavor to draw forth from the Divine Source equally, or does not wish to do so.

We would say the same concerning the life beyond, if the soul had the freedom to choose the good or evil as it has in its life on earth. But the soul has no such freedom there. Moral testing of every human being ends forever with physical death.

The condemned soul feels remorse, but repentance does not effect moral advancement there because the arena of activity for moral behavior in which the soul may prove its moral advancement in a practical way does not exist anymore, not after the death of the body.

The partial judgment of every soul by God takes place upon the death of each person, and it is then when it is decided which shall be its place on the Ladder of Blessedness or its place on the Ladder of Condemnation.

Therefore, for a soul, the drawing of more or of less blessedness in the life beyond the grave does not depend in the least, henceforth, on its desire, but only on the degree of the place which (according to its moral value) it has in the series of moral stature, i.e., it depends on how much receptive power the soul has from its life on earth in order to receive happiness from the Divine Source in Hades.

According to the Divine Scriptures, the saints who were the most faithful keepers of the Divine Will are nearer to the Throne of the Supreme Being surrounded by Angelic Orders and from whom begins the life of those in the Place of Comfort. The nearer the place of a soul is to the Source of Light, the Son of Glory, that much greater does it have the blessedness that is sent forth as rays of light and comfort from the Divine Source.

Together with other characteristics which Holy Scripture mentions as comprising or contributing to the happiness of the devout souls beyond the grave is the viewing of God, the Beatific Vision, i.e., the devout persons shall see God face to face. But we had concluded that the soul will be receptive of blessedness according to its place in the series of good deeds and according to its nearness to God. It is, therefore, obvious that this bliss and beatitude of a soul depends on how much or how little it sees God. In other words, the farther its position is from the Throne of God, the less the soul will see God, because its moral power is less and that much less will its blessedness and bliss be in the world beyond. And where a great distance separates the soul from God in this series, it loses completely its ability to see God. There also is the boundary between the Place of Comfort and the Place of Torment. There is where beatitude and bliss end. And from that point on is the beginning of the great chasm and the Place of Torment. The light and warmth from the Divine Source are no longer perceived by the souls that are there because their sinfulness has annihilated their ability to be receptive. Darkness and the gloom of Hell begins from that point.

Since a soul sees God and receives from the Sun of Glory unfading light and warmth of sweet divine reflection, which gives it beatitude and bliss, it is natural that when a soul is deprived of these and remains in a freezing gloom, far from fully feeling the presence of God, it is in torment, affliction, and dejection. The hopelessness of a condemned soul increases proportionally as its position goes higher and higher in the scale of sinfulness and naturally farther away from the Source of Light and Beatitude.

But for a soul to see God and to communicate with him

in the world beyond and receive satisfaction from his reflected glory is the same thing, as we said elsewhere. This comprises the *religious pleasure* of a devout person in his life on earth. The only difference is that in the world beyond the pleasure is greater, more satisfying, because the soul there is a spirit whose senses are clearer and whose impressions are more vivid. And since on earth only a part of satisfaction of pleasure was given to a devout person, surely in the life beyond the supplementation of this pleasure is reward and satisfaction. And, on the contrary, the souls that did not have this religious pleasure in their earthly life will neither have it in the Place of Torment, as we had seen above, but will feel its absence terribly. Because as a spirit the soul in Hades, in the Place of Torment, has clear senses which were dimmed by the demands of the body in its earthly life. Consequently, it feels there the loss of Divine Grace which it did not feel while on the earth. It feels the impression more vividly because the lure of covetous greed and all-devouring egoism and individuality that made it insensible in life are now dimmed. And the soul in Hell, liberated from all these things that had captivated it on earth and did not allow it to seek and have religious pleasures on earth, feels a great desire for satisfaction in the world beyond because it is so far away from the Source of satisfaction; it feels terrible dejection because it is so far from the Source of Light. And it feels horrendous hopelessness because it is far from the Source of Blessedness.

If this is not the punishment for the condemned and callous souls in Hades, I do not know what kind of punishment, a boiling pot, or a lake of material fire, would be, for it is impossible to know how a spiritual being could burn in a material object.

But this kind of punishment, which is also suitable for demons, is not opposed to the mercy of God. It is not an imposition of external torments imposed by God as another Torquemada of the Holy Inquisition. Rather, it is the result of the place that the human being himself prepared for his life beyond the grave, and from the natural sensitiveness that each soul, good or evil, has after its deliverance from its physical body.

A Narrative Example: A very rich but unmerciful man had not given any help to anyone during all of his life, except for a few rotten boards from his storage room to a poor man for his fireplace. When he died the angel of death led his soul to a deserted place where there was an old hovel, small as a doghouse, made of termite-ridden wood. "This is where you will stay forever," said the angel. The soul of the rich man protested, claiming that it was too small and, besides, it was made of rotten wood. "Yet," answered the angel, "what can we do about it: That was all the material you gave us when you were on earth, to fix your house here."

CHAPTER THREE

Does the Soul Progress in the Next Life?

To this question I answer that many theologians, and not only of the Roman Catholic and the Protestant churches but even of the Greek Orthodox Church, from olden times until today, have expressed the opinion that the souls in Paradise undergo moral improvement, while those in Hell undergo a moral deterioration until they reach a final degradation, or even improvement as in Paradise.

If, with what they call "moral improvement,"[12] they mean that the souls there graduate on the vast series of meritorious works from one position of blessedness to a better one, this is not based on Holy Scripture nor does it stand logically.

But if we accept that the souls of the devout in Paradise, having no concern over moral improvement, do nothing, then we must accept that they exist in a passive state, without actions and life. But I doubt that such a passive state, even if it experiences blessedness from the Source of Bliss and lives up to the Divine Creation of the soul which endowed it with so many abilities in its life, would have any purpose.

For this reason, I think that we should look to other means of bliss which are also given by God to devout souls. With the other means that we will mention, the soul is put into motion: an occupation, an activity, is given life. Towards this purpose, we must refer to the previous pages where we showed abundantly that there exist in the world beyond intellectual, aesthetic, and sentimental pleasures for the souls. Furthermore, these pleasures are clearer, more beautiful, and more satisfying than they are here on earth.

As we all know, the ability that a person has here on earth to have such pleasures depends on the intellectual, aesthetic, and artistic interests and abilities of his temperament. One might have poetic tendencies, another architectonic, another philosophic, another musical, another mechanical, while someone else may have none of these tendencies at all, and is a street-cleaner, a shepherd, or an undertaker, etc. This ability depends on some conditions of how each person was brought up and the kind of life he has led. One might have had an inclination for sculpture and yet was brought up to be a fisherman, and his talent was never expressed. But over there, in the life beyond the grave, the ability of his soul to accept and have such pleasures is given to all human beings. But it is given to each soul according to the place it will have in the ladder of its accomplishments. Thus, the little or great bliss that a soul will have there in the world beyond is also included in the measure and kind of rewards that the devout and good souls will receive there, i.e., those who are worthy of reward. For this reason, such pleasures, intellectual, aesthetic, and sentimental, shall be had by all, not only by the human beings who had them on earth. But the souls of those worthy of reward, who did not have any such pleasures in this life, will also have them. The latter will also have such intellectual, aesthetic, and artistic sentimental pleasures in the world beyond:

a. Because all souls without exception are endowed with a sense of the good, the beautiful, and the true. And it matters not that for one reason or another they do not have the opportunity to express them in earthly life.

b. Because these pleasures comprise the reward for the souls worthy of reward, in the life of the world beyond. And since each soul there has the ability to more or less enjoy such pleasures, which depends on the degree of worthiness, i.e., on the moral stature that he had in this life, it is neither just nor logical that a soul worthy of reward should be deprived of these pleasures in the world beyond just because for one reason or another it did not have them here in this life.

Therefore, every soul in Hades will be able to enjoy such pleasures according to its worthiness and not according to the inclination that it had in such occupations and pleasures in this life. It is possible for the soul of a great artist to have less bliss in the aesthetic pleasures in the world beyond than the soul of an undertaker who never in his life had the least idea of aesthetic, artistic pleasures. This may happen if the moral quality of the undertaker is greater than the moral quality of the artist, because the soul of such an undertaker in the life beyond the grave will be closer to the Source of Blessedness than the soul of the artist who was less moral than the undertaker.

But the ability of the soul to receive more or less bliss from the intellectual and aesthetic occupatons in Hades is proportional to the worthiness. This does not mean that it will receive these pleasures as a non-living inactive soul. It will be occupied with them, it will act, it will live in those noble intellectual, aesthetic, and sentimental pleasures, and it will be able furthermore to enhance the cycle of the activity of these occupations.[13]

This, however, will not give the soul more bliss and blessedness than what is proper to it according to its moral stature, because within the limits of its worthiness is included the reward which will come to the soul from its occupations. And the cycle of its activity will not be boundless, so that its bliss may be limited more than what it should be.[14]

It is possible for a soul to have progress in activity in the world beyond without rendering it more blessed than what it deserves to be according to its worthiness. Each soul worthy of reward will enjoy the intellectual and aesthetic occupations beyond the grave and will increase its knowledge of the infinite mysteries of the universe that it discovers with its occupation. But this will not disturb the line of moral worthiness of the souls there and, therefore, the blessedness of each one will be exactly as much as the partial judgment of God determined for it, regardless of how much the soul is occupied with the intellectual and aesthetic pleasures of the world beyond.

From all that we have said, the conclusion is that without being obligated to accept that there is moral improvement of the souls in Hades, which would destroy the moral purpose of the soul in this life here on earth, we can accept that there is progress in the life of the soul, with a greater and greater widening of its horizons and a continual extension of its boundaries. Here the soul acts, is occupied, and lives actively and not passively or inert, as if paralyzed in an inactive, blessed, oriental, satiated life in the world beyond.

Those intellectual and aesthetic pleasures that give bliss as a reward to souls worthy to be rewarded in the world beyond are completely denied to the condemned souls there. This deprivation is also a punishment that brings to the souls a great unquenchable thirst. And this deprivation is severely felt there, not only by condemned souls which on earth had intellectual and artistic pleasures, but also all the other souls that had not felt such beauty in the world. They also will feel this deprivation in Hell because, as we said previously, all the souls are endowed with the sense of the good, the beautiful, and the lofty.

However, I wish to make one observation concerning the sentimental pleasures that come to the life from the love of parents for their children, and the love of the children for their parents, marital as well as brotherly love, and, in general, love for relatives and friends. We said that such pleasures will exist in the world beyond. But the place where the relatives or friends will go may not be the same. It is possible for a father to be in Paradise and his son in Hell. A sister in Paradise and a brother in Hell. A husband in Paradise and his wife in Hell. In such instances, since they do not meet nor live together, the devout soul in Hades will enjoy bliss, but also pain, because it does not have with it the loved ones of earthly life or even because they are suffering in the Place of Torment.

And certainly we will accept this, if we consider the matters of the world beyond with a measure of improvised logic. But when we have in mind the Holy Scriptures, that the worthy souls have a cloudless sky in the life beyond the grave and that "there is no pain, sorrow, or suffering," it becomes necessary for us to examine the matter a little deeper.

Does the Soul Progress in the Next Life? 79

Previously we said that the occupations, intellectual and aesthetic, of a soul worthy of reward in Paradise, as much as they are pleasant, do not change its place and they do not give greater blessedness and bliss than that which is its due according to the partial judgment of God for its worth. In the same manner, therefore, the impressions which it has from the knowledge that its loved ones are far away, indeed in the Place of Damnation, as sorrowful as we might imagine them to be now, shall not lessen, nor influence at all, its blessedness there.

If we accept that such sorrow will lessen the blessedness and happiness of the souls that are worthy of reward in the world beyond, then we will arrive at the most absurd conclusion, that the happiness of the souls in Paradise is not proportionate to its worthiness, but that it depends on how many sinful relatives and friends it has. If a devout soul has many but sinful loved ones, then its blessedness will be negated and our moral life on earth will be worthless and will not contribute to bliss in the world beyond, because other persons were or are sinful in their earthly life. But this would be intolerable.

The matter is accordingly the same for Hell and the condemned souls. For a condemned soul, the idea that loved ones are in Paradise does not moderate the trial of torment. Nor does it increase its maliciousness or give it joy and happiness, on the other hand, from the fact that persons that it hated are also there and perhaps in worse torment.

CHAPTER FOUR

Explanations

We gave a meager idea concerning the rewards and punishments in the world beyond which our faith here allows us to have, looking through the small apertures between the bars of the doors of Hades. And referring back to the basic matter, "if untimely death is horrible, cruel, and unjust," we have the answer that for the devout, not only is it not such but, on the contrary, it is a desirable terminal to which the devout souls, with a justified hopeful expectancy, look forward to reach as soon as possible, as the Apostle Paul says in his Epistle to the Philippians:

> My desire is to depart and be with Christ, for that is far better (Philippians 1.23).

For the impious, however, and those worthy of punishment in general, truly death is horrible, a very unwanted visitor, an inexorable avenger. But, in this case, the question again arises: Is it not absolutely justified that people fear death which is for them a horrible matter? Are not the lamentations, wailings, and sobbings of persons justified who love those that have died, since, indeed, it is a known fact that the punishable persons are more than the devout? The answer is a great NO. They would be justified for this:

    a. if each person who will be condemned was preordained beforehand for Hell, regardless of his will and his actions;

    b. if the demands of the merit-worthy life was greater than those that a person was able to do; and

    c. if every sin of man, every straying of his life, was not subject to correction in this world so that, once a person committed a sin, he would be irreparably condemned, no matter how much he repented.

This study would not have any value if we did not

Explanations

examine, even with a casual glance, these three topics in order to determine if one is justified in reproaching death, for the reason alone that death leads us to a condemned life beyond the grave.

a. MAN IS A MORALLY FREE BEING

The life here on earth is a testing of the soul, an education and preparation of the spiritual existence of a person. It would be of no value since we have moral laws and try to practice them if the effort and the sacrifice of the individual did not contribute at all towards the success of putting them into practice. Any religion that would regulate the moral acts in life without allowing freedom of action would be taboo, superstition, a wretched device to tyrannize man in this life. If God was such a one as to regulate arbitrarily who will be the good in life and who will be the evil ones, and, according to such a decision, give some persons all the facilities to gain the good things, and to others only the evil, and then again, according to this scenario, to reward the former in the world beyond while he punished the others, then our idea of God would be absurd.

Since this entire study concerning death is based not on rationalism but on the Christian view, then this is its purpose: to teach the readers. Again, according to the Holy Scriptures, we also will briefly examine the topic of moral freedom of man.

If, in Christianity, a person does not have the freedom to choose the good from the evil, then the teaching of Holy Scripture is reduced to a blank paper.

The Sermon on the Mount of Jesus would resemble the admonition of a father who advises his son not to catch a cold, while, in the meantime, he sends him unclothed out of the house in freezing and stormy weather so that he will catch a cold. The Gospel Parables would be merely philosophical idle talk.

The death of Christ on the Cross would have value for only a small section of mankind — the lucky or the arbitrarily select, i.e., Herod, Pilate, and the Archpriests, etc., in the New Testament, would be irresponsible executors of a tedious and thankless job which was assigned to them by God.

But the Christian, for whom this study was made, accepting Holy Scripture, should inevitably accept that man chooses freely to do good or to do evil, and that each one is responsible for the kind of selection he makes. Therefore, when we prefer the evil instead of the good in our earthly life, it is not just to consider death which terminates life even untimely, as horrible, and to justify ourselves for this opinion with the idea that he who dies will go to hell and be punished. This is not justified because, after all, that sinful person would die sometime. A few more years of a sinful life would not in the least make him die more happily.

And, indeed, if we take into account the sinner's inclination towards evil, when the longer he lives the more he usually delves into sin, then death, coming untimely, becomes his benefactor, that is, it comes before the sinner might become corrupt and completely callous.

b. IS MORAL LIFE VERY DIFFICULT?

The sincere answer to this question is as follows: For an individual to live in society with a family, and have family responsibilities and occupational obligations, and, at the same time, to succeed, to progress, to distinguish himself as everyone desires, this makes moral life very difficult. If this were easy, it would have been something common and not worth the effort to talk about, as if it were of special great merit.

Moral life is difficult living in society because most of the physical pleasures and leisures (which, up to a point, favor the welfare of the body) are satisfied, for the most part, by general or partial violation of the moral laws. Moral life is difficult because rising in some positions (which indirectly contributes to betterment in life) is very slow moving when the individual seeks it with his own personal worth alone. Often his worth is put aside by the skillful ones who use devious methods. Thus, it becomes necessary for a worthy person, in order to succeed, to use these same methods,

Explanations

which, for the most part, are transgressing or mutilated practices of the moral laws. Moral life is difficult because family obligations and urgent needs make a person lose his patience and his serenity, and they lead him blindly to deeds that are not strictly Christian, nor socially just.

But the fact that moral life is difficult does not mean that it is impossible, nor that it is beyond the powers of a naturally and intellectually endowed average person.

All the instances I mentioned are needed and sought after by all kinds of people, but they are not indispensable in life, nor are they always a source of happiness. And although most of these are good and contribute to the progress of individuals (which also means the progress of society), and they should be sought after, if the acquisition of them leads away from the moral life, it is preferable to acquire less by legal means, or to disregard them completely.

Indeed, if one were to disregard even the additional and unnecessary needs of life, one would feel the consequences and would be embittered and would sob and cry. For this reason, those who rose or were raised above these needs of physical life and disregarded them completely became spiritual heroes and attracted attention and admiration and, in the language of Christianity, are called — Saints. Even though these should be the polar star of the voyage here on earth for all of us, and their example to be the compass of our ship of life, nevertheless we recognize the fact that it is not easy for all of us to be like them. But there are an infinite number of degrees of moral life, commensurate with the abilities of each person and the conditions of his life. Let us be satisfied with whatever our moral efforts will provide for us as long as they are sincere.

This also requires effort and patience in the selection of the methods which will support each of us in one of these moral degrees. This is up to us and it is not very difficult. If we do not choose to struggle at all, we are worthy of our evil fortune after death.

c. IN SPITE OF ALL OUR EFFORTS, WE STILL SIN

Indeed, this is the truth. But what of it? Our Savior Jesus Christ has provided especially for this, for he knew, as no one else who had lived on earth, the weaknesses of human nature. It is indisputable that sin is forever before each of us regardless of how devout we may be. We have examples of holy men who, in a weak moment, stumbled on sin and fell into it and, in falling, were bruised spiritually. Our Lord and Savior looks with paternal pain, kindness, and unbounded sympathy as we stumble and fall into sin, and yet if we remain satisfied or unconcerned about sin, this is unforgivable. There is no justification for this. When the soul arrives in the boat of death on the other side of life, then the partial judgment of God will not count how many times that that soul fell into sin, but how many opportunities for repentance and return to grace it scorned for even one sin that it committed. For this reason, the Apostle Paul, in his Epistle to the Ephesians, writes:

> Awake, O sleeper, and arise from the dead and Christ shall give you light (Ephesians 5.14)

And our Lord said in the Gospel according to St. Luke:

Just so, I tell you, there will be more joy in heaven over one sinner who repents than over ninety-nine righteous persons who need no repentance (Luke 15.7).

It is true that the life of a person is a slippery incline and he falls into sin, but that is not what regulates the place of the soul in the life beyond the grave in the series of the condemned in the gloom and the calamity in the Place of Torment instead of in the joyful series of those worthy of reward in the Place of Blessedness. It is the persistent and miserable disdain we show for the paternal love of God and that, knowingly, we prefer continuously the sinful state instead of repentance and spiritual cleansing.

And although a person should be always be ready, yet

the opportunities, by far and often, are given by God, even up to the last moment in which Charon signals for a person to make ready because his time has arrived. Even at the eleventh hour of life, our Savior Jesus Christ will accept our sincere repentance and reward us, as well as the person who, by great struggles in life, willingly strayed away a little. Jesus said to the repentant thief on the cross:

> Truly, I say to you, today you will be with me in Paradise (Luke 22.43).

only a short time before he died. We should not make such a postponement deliberately by saying: "now that I am young, I will transgress every law, and when I grow old, I will have the time to repent."

If, in spite of all this, a person dies unrepentant in sin and his soul is dragged by its own grime into the stifling gloom and anguish in the Place of Torment, is one justified in blaming death because it came too early? And are the sobbings and lamentations justified when they are caused by the idea that in death a person goes from this happy and pleasurable world to the Place of Torment?

AND NOW THE CONCLUSION

The material world in which we live is a place in the universe in which there exists another world, the world of spirit. The one, the material world, is temporary, perishable, and at some time will be destroyed. The other world is unchangeable, eternal.

The material world, even though perishable and temporary, has inexhaustible and priceless beauties most suitable to make man happy, who was created by God to be its master. And man is master of the material world because he is a being superior to everything else that lives in it. Man was created by God of two elements. The one was material, an earthly body, an element compatible to the surrounding material, earthly world, so that he would be able to adapt himself completely to it. The other is the spiritual element, or breath of divine breathing, a soul, suitable for the other higher world, the world of the spirit, the world of souls. And, for this reason, the life of man is a material-spiritual one, but separated into two sections in accordance to the life of the two worlds. The one section is called the terrestrial life, perishable, temporary, just like the world in which it resides. The other is called the spiritual life, imperishable, eternal like the world of spirits.

Human nature was created according to the beauties of the two worlds. It is, e.g., endowed by God abundantly, rich with potentialities that make it feel the beauties of the terrestrial life and be happy. And, further, it is endowed with the needs of the body, the animalistic lower ones such that when a person satisfies them with the proper means, they provide many pleasures. The purpose, however, of these abilities is to make human beings able to feel and appreciate the beauties of the other life in the world beyond, in the sphere of the world of spirits, the world of higher beings, the spiritual world. And since terrestrial life is temporary, and the world beyond is eternal, it is logical and natural, e.g., terrestrial life should not hinder the development of the human being on the road on which it will become suitable for the eternal life in the world beyond. And much more, it should contribute to this. In other words, the material life should serve as a preparation for the later spiritual life.

For this to happen, however, man himself should want this. He himself should want his terrestrial life or earthly life to be such that it should be a suitable preparation for the world beyond. If this were to depend directly on God alone and we were to receive this development in a passive manner, the gradual development of a fleshly-spiritual being would have been completely unnecessary. Surely God could have created us, from the beginning, higher spiritual beings, as the angels are. Therefore, our will is also necessary for our development. Development means motion forward or upwards. Will means action, endeavor. But that endeavor for motion, progress, requires again suitable election of the way and the means to success. The suitable means with which a person will use his terrestrial or earthly life so that his development and his existence which prove him to be suitable for the beauties of the life in the world beyond are called "moral means," and the way is called the "moral life."

God did not abandon man to himself in the selection of the moral means. He showed them to him himself. He wrote on the human heart some safe and unchangeable beautiful laws. He further sent successively wise and inspired men who spoke to mankind concerning these laws and brought them to its attention. Among all peoples, in general, there appeared in the course of the centuries such inspired men sent by God who in some places were called "wise" and in others "prophets." And finally God sent his only-begotten Son, not mere man, but the God-man, who besides shedding his Blood on the Cross for the redemption of man, taught the whole truth.

(Before the coming of the Redeemer) if man had followed the teachings of the inspired men sent by God, the wise men and the Prophets, he would have put into practice in his terrestrial (earthly) life the suitable means, that is, the law written by God in the human heart and the laws that were given through Moses and the divinely inspired Prophets. Those laws, together with the illumination that the souls would receive in the world beyond from the preaching of the God-man in Hades, would have been sufficient to develop man's being into a higher spirituality suitable for the spiritual life in the world beyond.

If man, after the coming of the Redeemer, will follow his teachings, faith, works, and sanctification, he will be able with these alone to develop his being to a more spiritual degree suitable for the world of higher beings, the world of the noble spirits. Mistakes are easy for man, but also easy is the correction, for as many times as they occur and for as great as they may be, the correction is simply sincere repentance.

The time limit for the preparation of the soul is the termination of earthly life. The final time, after which immediately begins the other stage and the life in the world beyond, is called "death."

If the effort for preparation was made, and made successfully, then death is the gate to the entrance into eternal Blessedness. If the preparation was not made, then death is the brink of the abyss. But even though a person should always be prepared, however, for this reason, even in the eleventh hour, if he will repent and prepare, he will not fall short of the others.

The pleasures of earthly life that are the result of the beauties of this world and of the satisfactions of the needs of the body, even the carnal needs, bring absolutely no hindrance to the efforts for preparation. The terrible hindrance is the unlawful use of these, and the abuse, that on one hand condemns a person to an animalistic condition and makes him its slave and, on the other hand, makes him an idolater and one who scorns God.

Enjoy life, O Christian, with its noble beauties and pleasures, but enjoy them conscientiously in a Christian manner. Your soul will continue such a life in the life of the world beyond, and with greater beauties and pleasures, strewn bountifully to every worthy soul.

Then death will become your best friend which, even though you never need to seek it, when it comes to meet you, you will embrace it with joy in your eyes.

Notes

1. Because we prefer not to answer does not mean that we are trying to evade the issue from a lack of arguments. The matter of the immortality of the soul, according to which after the death of the human body, the soul continues to exist, as its personal existence, is a matter of metaphysics. It belongs, that is, to religion and philosophy. But when a conversationalist does not believe in the opinion of religion, which is an undebatable doctrine that is not subject to questioning, and yet wishes to discuss it philosophically, such a discussion will never truly end. Because in a philosophical discussion there is never a final victor, since it becomes a matter of "beating the air" in which each speaker has his own "beater," his own personal arguments and logic. All the wise men of the world of all ages, more or less, have occupied themselves with this topic, some for and some against it, and yet no one yet has said the final word in which there is no room for one more negative argument. Consequently, we do not avoid a discussion with those who accept non-existence, the complete loss of human existence after death, for fear lest we shall be defeated. Rather we prefer not to answer only because the nature and purpose of these lessons demand it. Just as in my previous study, "Why Should a Pious and Good Person Suffer in Life?," so also this book was written for the Orthodox Christian families for the purpose of expressing in it the teachings of our Orthodox faith in regards to the mysterious problem of human existence concerning the life beyond the grave. It is not a study in Apologetics.
2. I repeat that the purpose, just as in the reason, for writing is to prove to the Christian that he should look at death without fear. When one looks at death in this manner with trust, without confusion of his mind or terrified because of a false notion concerning death, he may at least in the time of danger, prepare himself spiritually and not lose, as many now do, the final opportunity to save his soul.
3. Even untimely death, indeed, is natural death if we should

examine it closely as the result of certain chemical changes which occur in the animal organism from toxins and destructive germs that react under favorable conditions. But we do not wish to enter into biological theories because here we are not concerned with how death occurs. Rather, we take it as an event which occurred because of some cause. Then again, there is death that results instantaneously from an accident, drowning, shooting, a fall from a height, automobile or train collisions, or the like. Inasmuch as it occurs in these instances, some violent natural change takes place, and perhaps at the moment that it takes, we separate it from death that comes naturally, death by old age, which is unavoidable.

For this reason, when we mention natural death, we shall mean death from old age alone. The other death that results from unexpected sickness or accident we shall call *untimely,* even though it may occur in old age.

4. A realistic description of the condition of man in old age is given to us by Dr. M. Krenderopoulos in his book titled "The Book of Love, Woman, and Death," published by the firm "Grammata" in Alexandria. He says: "Although theoretically old age should begin from the moment when development stops, i.e., at age 25, usually much later, about age 40, agility of the joints and the rapid adaptation of the muscles of movement decreases, the skin loses its elasticity and generally the organism presents less resistance to external influences, and cohesive tissue develops more and causes that which the doctors call hardening of the arteries with all its consequences. As the years proceed, the hair whitens and falls, movement becomes difficult, the knees fold, the joints harden, the back curves, and finally a general collapse occurs, which is the preface of death.

The misfortunes of old age are not restricted only to the body. Old people suffer spiritual changes which are their greatest torment. They feel that the role they were destined to play in this world has ended, or is about to end. They think that the others reproach them for the place they still occupy, and for this reason they distrust everyone and they detest everything that is new and has abundant life. Every hour that passes brings to them new wrinkles. Every moment adds new griefs to their bitterness. Their imagination has stopped being flexible and they live with the memories that the present dims. The years follow one after the other and they become more misanthropic, more egoistical, and more life-loving. If there are a few whose heart throbs with emotions, it throbs in breasts afflicted and ready to crumble. If a few still retain youthful dreams, they always are broken on the cliffs of their weaknesses, just as the wave breaks on a rocky seashore. If they have desires and appetites, they are obliterated like bubbles at the creaking of their bones. There is no doubt that old age is a compulsory sickness and unavoidable from wherever it may come, whether its cause is external, or if it arises from the depths of the organism.

5. The oyster lives and dies in the sand and has no other pleasure in life than eating and perhaps twice a year of satisfying its sexual drive. It also protects itself as much as possible when danger threatens its life. And if someone should say that even food alone, after all, is pleasure enough for the animals, I would answer that there are animals for whom food is not easy to find. The pangs of hunger and what they suffer from hunger is so great for some that it is impossible for the little food they might find here and there to satisfy them. And yet an animal under such circumstances again will defend itself with any weapon with which nature endowed it against every danger which might threaten its life, even at the moment when it is desperate because of hunger and we would think that if it could talk, it would say at that moment, "Come and kill me and get it over with as soon as possible so that I can be relieved." It is the feeling of self-preservation which forces it to defend itself in order to extend its life, even under these miserable conditions.

6. Take a look at the prisoners sentenced for life and especially in earlier times, when the prisons were caves or deep cellars in forts without much light, without fresh air, where they were held there with shackles on hands and feet, completely isolated day and night for ten, fifteen, twenty years or more, without absolutely any pleasure. Without food often, except for a piece of dry bread each day, and once in a while a dish of poorly cooked legumes and a little water from an old tin can, and often suffering from fever and tuberculosis. If we disregard the hope that they had that they would be released someday soon, and the deceptive thought that the instinct of self-preservation gave them, what else did they have to make

their life worth living? In reality, death would have been incomparably preferable as a means to a future more just life, even as a final non-existence to nihilism, which, after all, would not have the tortures of the present life.

7. Certainly it is possible for some to ask: Since souls are without bodies and, as spirits, occupy no area, expanse, space, or place, how does it happen that they remain in some place? This question is natural. There is, however, the answer that the idea that we have here on earth concerning space and place should not be used in our thinking to judge the invisible world's space and place in infinity because we do not know the conditions of their relationships. Even in the mundane world concerning time, we do not have a clear idea, and we use the system of seconds, minutes, hours, days, months, years, even though scientifically there exists another system of time which is inconceivable to the masses. (See, "Man the Unknown" by Alexis Carrel).

Furthermore, if we accept the idea that the souls do not exist in some definite space, we will fall into two very false conclusions: a. that the human soul is infinite and unlimited, although only God is such, because only one infinite and unlimited being can exist. If we accept the idea that there are many infinites, then none of them are infinite. The one would limit the others; and, the souls of the sinners would not be separated in the life after death from the souls of the just and good. This is rejected by Holy Scripture, as proven above.

8. In the previous chapter, we saw that the soul does not terminate its relations neither with loved ones on earth, even though it leaves for the other world and they continue to live on earth, nor with the souls of those who had gone on before them. By continuing relations with these, the soul also retains the memory of the good deeds done on earth in relation to these persons and others. For these good deeds it is rewarded, i.e., it exists in the Place of Comfort. Furthermore, the soul feels and is sure that it truly is the same being, the same personality which, when in the physical body, did these deeds. All these together, we said, comprise the self-consciousness of the soul.

9. Some think that the ten talents are spiritual virtues. But this is a false notion, as we are assured by recognized great

interpreters of Scripture (Chrysostom, Homily 78 on the Gospel according to Matthew, and Homily 30 on the Epistle to the Hebrews, as well as Theophylact, commenting on the same chapter). We also see that the Lord gave one talent to him who was lacking in spiritual virtues. Therefore, the talents refer to native intellectual abilities, of which some have more and some less, and those with less, without harming the life of their soul in the least.

10. I will make special mention here concerning spouses. Regardless of how and why one person selects the other of the opposite sex with the decision to marry, regardless of how much love was in their heart before marriage, one thing is sure and indisputable for every sincere discussion, that the need for the fulfillment of the sex urge, if not the only, is yet the main incentive for marriage. For this reason, as much as the desire for a pleasant association is satisfied in marriage, or the need for showering love on children and grandchildren, or the mutual end of two persons in the struggles of life, who have deeply united their personal interests and have many other reasons to help one another, yet the harmony of marital life is greatly influenced positively or negatively by the warmth or the coolness of the conditions surrounding the satisfaction of their sexual needs. But in this, the temperament, health, character, the difficult struggles (beyond the abilities of the spouses) of life, defective or diligent upbringing, moral principles, environment, etc., of both, or at least of one of the spouses, contribute greatly. Therefore, that which is called marital love and which should provide noble sentimental pleasures in this life, in order to be preserved and expressed, has many dreadful obstacles which come to the surface, for the most part, from the time when the satisfaction of the sex drive is lessened.

For this reason, the sentimental pleasure that depends on married love here on earth is very doubtful or very fragile, and is often changed into a false hypocritical conditional expression of intent under which sometimes hate is hiding. But in the life of the world beyond things change. When the Sadducees asked our Lord Jesus Christ who would be the real husband of a woman who had taken seven husbands legally according to the Mosaic law, Jesus answered:

You are wrong, because you know neither the Scriptures nor the power of God. For in the resurrection (of the soul at the Second Coming), they neither marry nor are given in marriage but are like angels in Heaven (Matthew 22.29-30).

In other words, the souls there are not involved in carnal desires, and the difference between male and female does not in the least affect them. And since this is an assurance of Christ about life after the Final Judgment, when the resurrection of the bodies will also take place much more is this true concerning the Intermediate State of souls when they are bodiless.

Let us, therefore, take this literal assurance of our Savior Jesus Christ. Let us examine what enlightenment it gives us concerning the relations beyond the grave of persons who were husband and wife in life. If marital love, which should give the sentimental pleasures, did not give them, the reason is coldness, which comes from the lessening of the sex drive, which in turn terminates the sentimental pleasure. But since, in the life beyond, the grave marital communion and association does not include any satisfaction of carnal urges, it will be a love that does not entertain jealousy, satiation, or infidelity, but it will be an angelic love. It is natural that it will be an unclouded love which reflects the light of happiness as it is seen in children who, although they are boys and girls, display a pure love amongst them without the least hint of desire for carnal satisfaction.

11. It is logical that when someone is punished externally with instruments of torture, it is necessary that someone else punish and torture him. These writers assigned the duty of tyrannizing and punishing the sinners to the demons. In the descriptions and pictures of Hell, they show the sinners being punished there, but those who torture and tend the fires are holding pitchforks in hand and are the demons who are gleefully happy to carry out the work assigned to them. And thus we arrive at the absurdity that the devil, the most sinful being, the most hated by God, is enjoying himself in Hell, as the master in his sinister kingdom, having a job very much in accordance to his desires. While the sinful humans, who no matter how sinful they might have been, certainly were better than Satan, undergoing untold hardships by him.

12. There can be no moral improvement in the next world simply because there is no arena for moral exercise there. The soul, even without the participation of the body (as with thoughts of unbelief) can sin in life here. Generally, however, every spiritual sin here on earth is the result either of pressures of the body, or of limitations of the body and mental imperfections that hinder the soul to see the naked truth. Consequently, the soul participates with the body in every sin. And since in the next life the soul is there without the body, and so without its demands, it does not have, that which St. Paul calls:

> Another law at war with the law of my mind, and making me captive to the law of sin, which dwells in my members (Romans 7.22)

And, therefore, there is no war which it can win and advance morally. What then is that with which the soul can be tested to find it worthy to graduate?

Neither should we believe that that moral improvement in the next life is absolute predestination, that is, that God arbitrarily rewards or punishes, because this cannot be upheld by Christianity. However, if there were in the next life free testing of souls, such testing would certainly hide within it the great danger that the soul might fall from its place of blessedness. And if this happened, it would negate and make unnecessary and purposeless the partial judgment that God provides for every soul at the time the body dies.

Then again, if moral testing does not end when the body dies, but continues in the world beyond, why should this opportunity for improvement be given only to the good souls which have, after all, secured some happiness, and not be given to the condemned souls, rather than just allowing them to get worse. This false opinion of moral improvement of the soul in the life beyond the grave was based somehow on the following two thoughts which they support and say:

a. All those who died before Christ did not have the opportunity of learning about Christianity, the faith in the true God and the Christian moral law.

b. Millions and millions of people who lived after Christ belonged to other religions, i.e., Buddhism, Mohammedanism, Confucianism, etc., and, likewise, did not have the opportunity to become Christians.

Therefore, some say, that the opportunity should be given to the former and the latter to improve their moral condition beyond the grave. Furthermore, they say that Christ, during the three days that his Body was in the grave, went to Hades and preached the Gospel to them there, and that this was his purpose, to teach the Gospel law to the dead in Hades and save them. But this act of Christ either would save everyone there without exception, or a moral testing would take place, according to the law of the Gospel that was preached there in some manner. Therefore, there exists in Hades moral testing and moral improvement. That is what they say! To all this, however, the answer is the following: With the preaching of the Gospel in Hades by Christ, the souls there, good and evil, were enlightened and acquired the ability which every Christian human being has in this world by Holy Baptism. The souls in Hades did not have such ability there, just as they did not have it in their earthly life, as a result of original sin, before our Savior descended there to preach to them. With the preaching of the Gospel in Hades by Christ, neither were all the souls that were there saved, nor did any moral testing or moral improvement take place there. Only those souls were saved whose life on earth was such that if they were Christians they would have been saved. They are the ones that received the reward, i.e., they received the ability to feel the happiness which belongs to the good Christian souls after death, as souls of the just. Those souls, however, that, regardless to which religion they may have belonged, were perverse or unmerciful did not receive any better place even with the preaching of Jesus in Hades. They heard his sermon there, but again they remained punishable because they had broken the law, which naturally is written by God in the human heart. They are punished there according to the transgression of that law which they trespassed in this world.

We say the same concerning those of other religions who transgressed the Christian law without being guilty. They shall also be judged by the law written in their hearts by God and, consequently, less sternly, more mercifully. In other words, to them are applied the words of our Lord:

> But he who did not know and did what deserved a beating, shall receive a light beating (Luke 12.48), and

Woe to you, Chorazin! Woe to you, Bethsaida! for if the mighty works done in you had been done in Tyre and Sidon, they would have repented long ago, in sackcloth and ashes. But, I tell you, it shall be most tolerable on the day of judgment for Tyre and Sidon than for you (Matthew 11.21-22).

Therefore, moral improvement does not exist in Hades.

13. With what I now say, I do not wish to create new doctrines, nor do I wish to impose my thoughts on anyone, because they are not literal teachings of the Church. It is merely my theological opinion, just as there are hundreds of theological opinions which are taught in theological schools for the development of the science of Theology. And it is not impossible that they may prove to be unsupportable.

14. We shall delve into this a little deeper here, because I attribute great meaning to it. Therefore: It is a firm dogma of the (Greek) Orthodox Church that in the *Intermediate State,* that is, from the moment that the body dies until the Second Coming of the Lord Savior, the worthy souls in Hades have only a foretaste, a part of the bliss, that they will receive at the General Final Judgment. But this amount, the part of the entire bliss which God gives a soul, is not imposed on us to accept by any verse of Holy Scripture, i.e., that the soul will receive it entirely from the moment of physical death, and then that soul will remain inactive in its possession. This reward may be given gradually, and given by means of its pleasures that come from its occupation with its intellectual, aesthetic, and sentimental occupations, and to the degree that its worthiness allows.

A Concrete Example: Let us accept that the great astronomer Flammarion was a devout and good man in his life here on earth and that his soul in Hades, consequently, is worthy of reward. His reward will also consist, perhaps, of other satisfactions in the world beyond, such as religious, intellectual, aesthetic, and sentimental pleasures. Because Flammarion was an intellectual, let us limit ourselves to the intellectual pleasures which his soul will enjoy there.

Now it is not necessary that the amount of intellectual pleasures be immediately given completely to his soul there and, consequently, to immediately enjoy all the bliss that is derived from them. It is possible in every particle of time he be given consecutively a greater share of intellectual activity and occupations which give him pleasure and bliss. But while his soul, by this occupation, acts and progresses to greater circles of intelligence, the bliss that he feels does not necessarily become so greater, that it will exceed the limits of bliss which have been determined by his worthiness.

This also happens in this life here. A mathematician who has solved his first problem feels great pleasure. He will feel that much, and perhaps less, when he comes to solve a second and third problem. Even though he progressses intellectually and develops more with each pleasure that he feels going from problem to problem, it remains the same, and sometimes, indeed, it lessens, on the one hand, because he gets accustomed to these successes, and on the other, because the more he proceeds, the more he realizes his smallness before the vastness of total intelligence.

In like manner, the soul of Flammarion will be able to expand its knowledge of astronomy and to progress in the area of intelligence, and to enjoy it, but the bliss and blessedness from this will never exceed the boundaries of its worthiness, nor will it decrease.

And if a shepherd is as worthy as Flammarion, then his soul will be able to have the same amount of bliss as the soul of Flammarion, and yet his intellectual occupations in Hades might begin with the Pythagorian theorem and from there progress, but they will never attain to the occupations of the soul of Flammarion.